PEDAL TH

PEDAL THE PLANET

**One Man's Journey From The Depths Of Despair
To Winning The World Cycle Race**

Breifne Earley

8/12/16

To Charlie,

Enjoy the Journey,

Happy Birthday.

Breifne Early

BE PRESS

Published in 2016 by BE Press
Leitrim Village, Co. Leitrim, Republic of Ireland
Telephone: +353 83 4853420
Email: info@bepress.ie
Website: www.bepress.ie

First Edition

Book design and production by David Leeflang (CreativeHQ)
david@chq.com.au

Illustrations by Edel Feely
edel@outlook.ie

Cover Photograph by Jesse Horrelbeke
www.jalanpaul.com

Printed and bound by Walsh Colour Print, Castleisland, Co. Kerry
www.walshcolourprint.com

For Mamo & Aidan

1
MAN, INTERRUPTED

The drive back from the wedding had been three hours long. My only company in the car were the thoughts in my head, and they were getting louder and louder. As I got in the front door of the shared house I had a room in, I heard my flatmate pottering around in his room upstairs. I made my way to my bedroom before he might come out and I'd be engaged in pointless conversation with someone I couldn't stand to be around.

I craved the peace and quiet of my room, my sanctuary where I was able to really unwind and not worry about anything happening outside.

I knew that this time was different.

This time around, I wasn't going to be able to find peace and quiet anywhere, not in company and certainly not on my own. The voices in my head were screaming at me louder than ever before and they were repeating the same things over and over again:

"No one would miss you."

"The world would be a better place without you in it."

"No one loves you, you're just a burden to those around you, always negative."

"No one enjoys your company, they run a mile away from you."

All of these negative thoughts running around getting louder in my head. I heard the front door slam, knowing I had the house to myself again, I went to the bathroom.

Looking in the mirror, I barely recognised what I saw in my reflection. Grossly overweight, almost thirty years of age and with a heavy look of disappointment worn into my eyes, I could see why no girl had shown an interest in me for nearly two years; I hadn't exercised at all in almost five.

I'd attempted to get back into sport six months earlier but ended up fracturing my leg in two places on my first attempt at playing football. I'd failed to find a date for the family wedding the previous day, and my bosses were trying to sack me from my job. Everything in my life was at an all-time low.

I decided there was only one course of action: I needed to admit defeat, accept that everything in my life appeared to be so broken and past recovery. I should just throw in the towel and end my own life. I washed my face, too ashamed to look at myself in the mirror as I drew my head out of the sink and retreated to my bedroom.

I turned on the television in the corner of the room to try and drown out the voices in my head. I lay back on my bed to ponder the logistics of the task at hand. How would I do it? When? Where? What would I need to do? What would I include in a note? Before I could answer any of these questions, my phone started to vibrate on the locker next to the bed. As a reflex, I picked it up. There was a text message from my uncle:

"Next Sunday, the 10th of October 2010, is the twentieth anniversary of your cousin Michael Darragh's death. It's a pretty iconic date and our family will be holding a remembrance service for him in our house at 8pm. We would love your company."

Immediately my mind was flooded with memories of his funeral. I was three years younger than Michael Darragh. He'd been that older cousin who was usually the ringleader in any trouble that was going on, full of life and vitality. At 12, he'd been struck down with leukaemia and, within six or seven months of the diagnosis, he'd passed away. The devastation that it had caused in that branch of my family was complete and even twenty years later the scars of loss were etched into his parents.

I knew my own parents, twenty five years older than Michael's parents were then, wouldn't cope with my suicide. I'd effectively be sentencing them to a life of being imprisoned with their own thoughts.

"Could we have done anything to help Breifne?"

"Was any of this our fault?"

"Did we ignore any warning signs?"

It wouldn't have been their fault, not even a bit of it, but I knew that my parents, sisters and my two nephews would never be able to fully recover from what I had just decided to do. I didn't want to just pass my hurt onto them. I put my head on the pillow and closed my eyes.

2
THE BUCKET LIST

The voices in my head were silent for the first time in as long as I could remember. Then I heard the voice. Morgan Freeman's dulcet tones filled the room:

"Edward Perryman Cole died in May, it was a Sunday afternoon and there wasn't a cloud in the sky. It's difficult to understand the sum of a person's life, some people would tell you it's measured by the one's left behind, some believe it can be measured in faith; some say by love, other folks say life has no meaning at all. Me, I believe that you measure yourself by the people who measure themselves by you. What I can tell you for sure is that, by any measure, Edward Cole lived more in his last days on Earth than most people manage to wring out of a lifetime. I know that when he died, his eyes were closed and his heart was open."

I opened my eyes and looked at the television screen as the movie *The Bucket List* told the story of two terminally sick men played by Freeman and Jack Nicholson who became firm friends and helped each other discover themselves through completing a list of what they wanted to experience before kicking the bucket.

The range of their list included, amongst other things visiting the Egyptian pyramids, kissing the most beautiful girl in the world, laughing till they cried, helping a complete stranger for a common good and witnessing something truly majestic.

I was transfixed by the movie, and by one particular scene where Nicholson asks Freeman if he's ever considered suicide. They talk about it and decide that they're both in denial. I began to question whether I was also in denial about my role in each of the failed relationships I had in my life. My bosses, my ex-girl-friends, my friends and family, all seemed to be choosing to have little to do with me. When I looked at it objectively, I realised that for the most part it was largely my own fault. Over the two hours the movie played on the screen, an idea started to emerge.

I was going to write my own bucket list.

My start date would be obvious: Michael's anniversary would be on the tenth of the tenth, twenty-ten (10/10/2010). I decided to put ten items on my own list, ten individual but personal challenges which would, hopefully, turn my life in a positive direction.

I decided to redesign my life. I decided to do it by writing down what type of person I would like to be in a years' time. I asked myself what skills, habits or personality traits would I like to develop.

I knew that I needed to get fit, lose some weight, become more active and learn to cook for myself. I wagered that this was a huge factor in the lack of female attention, too.

I couldn't swim at all. This was a slightly irrational fear I'd had ever since a bad experience at the seaside as an infant had left me unable to put my head under water without panicking.

I had travelled extensively for work, but ten years after finishing school I couldn't remember the last time I'd taken an actual holiday.

Speaking of work, most of the negativity in my world seemed to come from my toxic work environment. My questioning of current management practices had set me on a collision course with the exit door.

In less than an hour, I had completed the list. I settled on a target finish date of the eleventh of the eleventh, twenty eleven (11/11/2011) and decided I needed an element of peer accountability so I posted the list to my Facebook page under the name "Challenge Ten".

The list in full was:

- Lose 30kgs in weight.
- Go on 50 blind dates.
- Perform in ten concerts / gigs.
- Save 10% of my annual salary in savings.
- Swim a total of 400m each and every week. Increase the distance by 100m each month.
- Visit 10 different countries.
- Cycle 50km each week.
- Attend ten cookery classes.
- Complete ten sporting challenges including a marathon, a triathlon and an open water sea swim.
- Apply for ten dream jobs.

I had just redesigned my life. I had my road map and I needed to take that first step.

3

THE PURSUIT
OF HAPPINESS

With one week to the start of my new life, I wanted to get a head start on the challenges I was now facing into. To get the ball rolling, I joined a gym and an online dating website, and I bought myself a diary.

At the same time, my Facebook account seemed to jump into overdrive with a massive volume of activity. Some people were offering me congratulations, some were calling me crazy, and a few offered some meaningful support. Two friends contacted me in that first week to offer me swimming lessons, and two more would join that list before the end of the month.

The first few days at work consisted of a lot of laughing at the lunch break, mostly at my expense. My colleagues seemed to believe that I wouldn't last a week before the list would be forgotten about. Most of their commentary revolved around the wisdom of saying I wanted to leave my place of employment before I'd secured somewhere else to go to.

*   *   *

The 10th of October rolled around and I woke up early that Sunday morning and drove to the gym for my first official weigh in and my first session. I planned a very simple routine of walking on the treadmill for five minutes as a warm up, then seventeen kilometres on the bike before hitting the pool and doing a bad imitation of a doggie paddle with my head out of the water from one end to the other until I clocked up seven lengths of the twenty metre pool.

Starting at just a few pounds shy of twenty stone (125kg), I was totally shattered half way through the cycling, which took me almost an hour to complete. It took nearly twenty minutes to manage the swimming element of the workout session before I was back in the dressing room questioning the entire project.

That evening in my uncle's home, surrounded by my extended family I could feel the love and support in the room. Twenty years since losing Michael Darragh, their loss and their pain were still as evident as ever. I knew I'd made the right decision the previous weekend and resolved to complete my list at all costs.

My first blind date was the following weekend, I met Kelly through an online service and we went for dinner. Sitting in the car five minutes early for the date felt so awkward. I was wondering if she'd show up, praying she wouldn't run a mile when she saw me, and scared that I might let myself down and want to flee on seeing her, worrying that we might have nothing to talk about. Her car pulled up and I took a deep breath and opened the door to greet her.

It all worked out perfectly, we had a lovely evening, the conversation flowed pretty much from the start and we both enjoyed it but no sparks or fireworks were anywhere to be seen.

* * *

The gym sessions, the dates, and the weight loss had started to have a visible effect, in terms of how I felt about myself but also in terms of how I felt I looked to the outside world. The gentle slagging around the lunch table had eased, and in its place was a genuine interest in my recent developments, particularly around my new-found dating life. The online blog I was maintaining had caught the imagination of my friends, family and colleagues.

I was en route to a date in Wexford when a radio conversation about online dating being for weirdos caught my attention. The Mexican girl, Ela, who I was meeting that day, had been on an online dating site when I found her profile earlier in the week. I sent a text to the show, taking exception to the negative portrayal of online dating and explaining my current set of challenges.

A few days later I got a call from the producer asking me if I'd like to come on the show the following week.

Chatting to the radio host, George Hook the following week about my plans was the first time I'd moved outside my immediate circle of friends with my story and the immediate response was phenomenal. Old friends and complete strangers reached out, messaged, tweeted and emailed me thanking me for sharing my story and wishing me luck with the year ahead.

4
EYE OF THE TIGER

At the end of the next week I fell in from work tired, sat down on the couch, turned on the television and, out of years of habit, I glanced over at the Chinese take-out menu hanging on the fridge. The temptation was almost overwhelming but my eye was caught on the training bag sitting in the corner of the room. It was that moment, when I got up from the couch, grabbed the bag and set off for the gym, that I knew I'd turned the corner. I was on a brand new trajectory.

My first sports event was the national indoor rowing championships, which my colleague Lisa had organised. I managed to recruit a team of thirteen friends to take on the challenge with me; most of them had never been in a rowing boat. Thankfully this event was held indoors, on rowing machines. We all featured in the lower reaches of our categories, although Fiachra ended up with a medal for his day out. Despite the herculean effort involved, we all had a great day and managed to raise a few hundred Euro for Paralympics Ireland in the process.

Over the Christmas period, I moved my training base back

home to Leitrim for a week or two, and bumped into my old football teammate Kevin and his wife, Bernie, at the swimming pool.

After their obvious shock at the sight of me exercising wore off, I was sharing my bucket list and my challenges with them, Bernie said, "Oh, just like Gerry Duffy." The name rang no bells with me. "Thirty two marathons in thirty two days, last summer".

I noted the name for later. Gerry seemed like someone I should be aware of, but I had no idea how big a part he'd play in my future.

I had selected a duathlon event in Naas, Kildare in late January for my next major sporting event. Two laps running around Punchestown race course were divided by a twenty kilometre cycle to Blessington and back. I borrowed a bike for the event and brought it down to the local bike shop to get it serviced.

When I explained to the guys in the shop what I wanted it for, they simply laughed. The rusted dual suspension mountain bike was totally unsuitable for the job at hand. I might as well turn up with stabilisers on the bike. They offered to rent me a hybrid bike that would suffice for the event. I happily agreed, relieved to have been spared embarrassment.

My friends Rob, Trish and Niamh agreed to join me for the duathlon and we got ourselves to the course about half an hour before the start time. Taking the bike out of the back of the car I heard my name called from across the car park. Sean, an old college friend, was walking towards me. He took one look at my bike and offered his help. He checked my tyre pressure and my brakes, and then wished me the best of luck. He expressed concern about the suitability of the hybrid bike and I didn't have the heart to tell him that I almost showed up with an even more pathetic steed than the one he'd seen.

Before we knew it we were off. As expected it took less than a half mile before I was struggling to stay with the crew. Niamh and Trish were already ahead, but Rob was hanging back with me. I had to stop as I just didn't have the legs.

Slightly embarrassed on Rob's behalf, I insisted that he continue to go at his own pace and not wait for me. The first portion of the run had been too quick for me, and now I was being passed by all the slow coaches who hadn't blown up behind me. The remainder of the lap was completed very slowly as I moved repeatedly from a walk to a run and back.

It was the first time I'd been on a bike outdoors since before I'd gotten my driver's licence nearly twelve years earlier. Where even the slowest people had been passing me and leaving me for dead on my feet a few minutes beforehand I was now enjoying a bit of the upper hand. I caught the first competitor as I neared the half-way point. As the cycle continued, I passed another dozen or so competitors including Trish and Niamh who really didn't appear to be enjoying the cycling aspect of the event.

Most of the people I'd passed on the cycle leg were beside me in what felt like no time at all. I managed to stay ahead of a number of competitors and thankfully didn't finish in last place although I was almost an hour behind the eventual winners.

My finishing position really didn't matter. I had completed the course. Another friend, Eamon, had waited at the finish line with a banana and a bottle of water, half an hour after his fellow speedsters had already left the premises. I appreciated that simple but significant gesture more than he will probably ever know.

The next two months saw repeat performances of the exact same event at the same venue. A steady increase in my speed and a decrease in the time it took to complete the course gave me a fantastic impetus to keep going on my journey. The running was getting a little easier, but it was on the bike where I was finding my real strength growing.

5

OFFICE SPACE

At the same time as my fitness levels and my self-belief increased, so did my bosses' efforts to remove me from my position. These troubles came from two directions.

A disciplinary process based on predominantly fabricated and utterly vague issues had been ongoing for six months. At the end of the process it was still unclear what exactly I'd been accused of.

Even the internal board member chairing my appeal hearing was unable to provide me with any specific information of any complainant or the complaints made against me.

At the same time, the executive board of my company sat down to agree on a new management role within the company.

On the day as I was interviewed for a promotion, I received an email informing me that I had lost my disciplinary appeal. If I hadn't suspected that I wouldn't get the promotion when I had applied, I certainly knew it when I entered the interview room and saw that one of the members of the interview panel had been the main contributor to the tensions over the years.

My instincts told me to fight against the constructive dismissal that was ongoing but the rational side of my brain weighed up the emotional cost involved in doing that and judged that it wasn't going to be beneficial. No amount of money would be worth the mental anguish that would follow for the next few months of dealing with this mess. I have no doubt that suicide would once again have become a very real prospect had I stayed in that environment.

I'd been approached with a number of opportunities for new employment and I'd applied for some amazing roles that crossed my radar. Eventually the opportunity to join a new start up called RateMyArea.com came up.

My cousin Ronan was leaving his position as the Head of Sales & Marketing with the company to travel, and he set up an interview with his boss for me to take over his role and head up their new daily deals website. The deal was done over a cup of tea and all that remained was for me to accept the role and serve my notice at my old job.

Instead of taking action, I wrote up my letter of resignation. It had never been about the money with me. I loved the work and it broke my heart to have to leave but I just couldn't stay in this environment.

I handed in my notice on my new boss' first day and started my holidays three days later, leaving him with no staff and no working knowledge of the organisation. I didn't care. I was on my way out.

6
SPLASH

My local bike shop, 2Wheels, and their sponsored rider, Mark Lacey, had taken me under their wing. Mark was a fitness trainer and he started me on a programme of running or cycling the two miles to the gym, and then taking part in an 8:00 AM spinning or aerobics class before showering and heading to work.

One morning, at the end of a particularly tough spinning session, Mark suggested I take part in an event that night. "Hellfire Duathlon" sounded like something I wasn't too keen on taking part in, but he convinced me that the word "Hellfire" just came from the name of a well-known ruined building on the route: I signed up.

I'd been doing a few duathlons in both Naas and Dublin's Phoenix Park so I figured I'd be able for it. Two three-kilometre runs either side of a seventeen-kilometre cycle was a shorter distance than what I was already doing.

What he hadn't told me was that while the Hellfire portion of the name did come from an old building, said building happened to be at the top of a steep hill in the Dublin Mountains. I made my way to the address Mark had given me and once I realised what I had let myself in for, I was completely petrified at what lay in store.

The race required me to run up and down a mountain twice before picking up my bike, then two laps of climbing up out of the valley, down the other side, and back up to the car park we'd started from. The ridiculously tough climbing and the even more scary descent on the far side were total eye openers for me.

By the time I'd finished with the bike at the car park, most of the runners had already completed their second run. Mark met me at the road and told me that I'd done enough. I shrugged him off and set off up the mountain. I was going to finish what I'd started.

It seemed to take forever, but as the ruin at the top of the mountain came into view for the fourth time I knew it was simply about getting back down the hill to the finish line.

It was almost totally dark when I crossed the finish line. The organisers and the marshals all waited for me to finish and they cheered me across the finish line. I had no doubt I got the best welcome of the night, albeit because the staff were probably just excited to be finished.

I'd only started learning to swim since October, and progress had been slow. I was able to get in the water, but putting my head under was still a very real fear of mine. Despite the best efforts of Martin, David & Richard who had each helped me at various stages to overcome this, I was still struggling.

I was just about able to complete a length at a time in the pool, but if anyone happened to be in the lane with me or even the feeling of the smallest ripple would send me into a panic and the resulting struggle was highly embarrassing.

I had set the challenge of competing in the Liffey Swim, a two mile challenge through the centre of Dublin. I was struggling to complete twenty five metres at this point, and I wasn't sure if I was going to make it or if I was crazy to even attempt it. I was facing into a challenge with actual safety concerns now. To say I was terrified was an understatement.

My friend and colleague David Malone, himself a former Paralympic Games swimming champion, pulled a few strings and organised a membership in his swimming club in order to be eligible to participate in the qualifying swims. In order to qualify for the Liffey Swim, you had to complete four swims.

This brought me to the end of the harbour wall at Dollymount Strand on Dublin's north side, facing a distance just over a kilometre back to the causeway joining the island to the mainland.

My friend Niamh tried her best to make me feel relaxed about the whole experience. She helped me get registered while I got my number and hat sorted. I was transfixed by the wide range of participants. People of all ages, shapes and sizes in swimming costumes walked around with confidence, most of their bodies on display.

Unlike me, they had no fear of comment on their physical make up at all. My old friend Larry appeared out of the crowd. He wished me well and tried to reassure me that I would be okay.

The race started, and within thirty seconds I knew I was in trouble. I gave up on the idea of trying to swim properly.

I was consumed with the taste of the salty sea water, the choppy waves and the wake of the swimmers who were passing me out.

The faster swimmers with the larger time penalties were all still to come from behind me. Like a knife through soft butter, they cut through the water so quickly that I had to wonder if they had actually just passed me or whether I'd imagined it.

Thirty minutes into what should have been a fifteen minute swim, I was just over the halfway mark. Trying to swim a free-style stroke without putting my face in the water was proving very tiring. I was really struggling, but I hadn't given up. One other swimmer who had been struggling maybe thirty metres ahead of me for the entire duration had called it a day just a few minutes earlier.

I heard my name being shouted from the sea wall to my right. Larry was there, waving at me. He had already finished his race. He dropped his bag, clambered down the rocks and eased himself back into the water. He was alongside me within a matter of seconds and stayed with me for the next twenty minutes as I struggled against the environment and the conditions, but mostly tried to cope with my own lack of ability and confidence in the water.

Eventually, after rounding the final buoy and covering the short distance back to the bridge, I felt the hard slimy steps beneath my hands and dragged myself up on the staircase, shivering but extremely proud of myself. I thanked Larry as we made our way to the bag drop area. My bag was the sole unclaimed item.

Needing four finished swims from the calendar to qualify for the Liffey Swim. I completed two more races at Seapoint and Malahide, while the strong tidal conditions in the Killiney race saw me pulled out of the water just after the half way stage. No matter how hard I swam, the tide was carrying me further and further from the course. Another attempt to complete the required fourth swim was cancelled due to adverse weather conditions, leaving me with no option but to enter for the Liffey Swim, listing the three completed events and explaining the reason for not having a required fourth qualifying swim on the list.

I wasn't permitted to race in the Liffey Swim that year, and it was probably for the best. I wasn't a strong swimmer, and the organisers had to keep both my safety and the safety of others paramount in their minds.

The sea swims I'd managed to finish had given me a little more confidence in the water, so when I joined the group gathered at the start of my first triathlon in Greystones, just a half hour south of Dublin, I wasn't totally out of my comfort zone.

I'd been focusing on the swim portion of the race in my half hour drive to the Wicklow town and I made a few decisions to help my anxiety levels. Firstly, I was wearing a wet suit for the first time, unlike the open water sea swim calendar, which forbids wetsuits, triathlons don't have the same restrictions.

The added buoyancy from the suit, along with the extra practice I'd had over recent weeks had me feeling much happier. I'd also decided to step back a metre or two and start my race behind everyone else. In the grand scheme of things it would make little to no difference to my time, but I'd avoid the scrum that traditionally starts these races. When the start was signalled, I waited for a few seconds and then once the initial excitement had eased I took off.

I surprised myself by not being the last person out of the water, in fact there were two bodies still windmilling away behind me as I hit the beach. Once again the cycle was fine. It was the run that cost me any hope of a respectable finish. I was still delighted just to finish the course.

Three weeks later, I repeated the performance, this time swimming the upper River Liffey and cycling and running through the Phoenix Park. Despite the swim including an upstream element, I comfortably emerged from the water ahead of a few bodies and managed to hold my own. I was still way down the field, but this was obviously a definite improvement from the first outing.

7
RATATOUILLE

One of my challenges had been to learn my way around a kitchen. I wasn't hoping to be Jamie Oliver or Gordon Ramsey, but it would be nice to confidently prepare a meal from scratch instead of sitting at home waiting for a delivery, or popping down to the chip shop for a burger. I took a few lessons and got myself a cook book, which I followed to the letter. I was really enjoying the satisfaction of being self-sufficient by preparing all my own meals. I also noticed the improvement in the fit of my clothing, with my ever reducing waistline making it easier to find clothes for myself too. Then my cousin Alan contacted me with a suggestion.

"I have a friend, Paul Treyvaud, who has a restaurant in Killarney, he's a bit mad though; he does videos about cooking quail in a tree, or pretending to hunt deer with a toy gun and then cooking the venison in the park. If you really want to learn to cook, he might let you work in his restaurant kitchen for a night. Want me to ask him?"

I immediately replied "Yes!"

Two weeks later, I found myself knocking on a door just off

High Street in Killarney, I was introduced to Mark, Paul's brother, who welcomed me into the kitchen and swiftly put me to work. My morning was spent preparing fish cakes for that evening's meals. After doing two samples Mark left me alone to finish the batch myself. I have a feeling after watching the first few he kept a pretty close eye on me from the other side of the room.

I might not have been offered a job on the spot by the Treyvaud brothers, but getting to watch the events unfold behind the scenes as the day progressed was fascinating. The processes and planning that goes into even just writing the menu was an eye-opening experience.

8
FORREST GUMP

My running had been stepping up in levels all summer. At the start of the year, I'd struggled to complete a mile. Six months later, I built right up to finishing the marathon series events with increasingly respectable times. I finished the five mile event in fifty four minutes, and the ten mile event in one hour, fifty two.

The final stretch of that race was a personal highlight. Still with energy in the tank and facing into a large climb up the Khyber Pass in Dublin's Phoenix Park, the long rise from beneath the Magazine Fort to the Papal Cross, I was flying by athletes who were obviously struggling.

Every person I passed was one place higher up the placings, one more person between me and my usual finishing place of last or second last in these types of events. The feeling of beating someone, anyone, felt great. My old competitive streak had been awakened, and I liked what I was seeing.

2Wheels had invited me to go to New Zealand during the Rugby World Cup that September to help raise money for the

IRFU's Charitable Trust.

After witnessing Ireland beat the Australians in Auckland, thirty Irish cyclists took to the mountains of the South Island and we cycled from Christchurch to Dunedin via the west coast and Queenstown. The main reason was to catch Ireland's encounter with Italy in the student town at the south of the island.

The experience was out of this world, in addition to the experience of seeing Ireland beat both Australia and Italy in the World Cup, we got to meet the players and had a special visit from head coach Declan Kidney. We also had the small matter of a 1,200 kilometre cycle, crossing the Southern Alps mountain range through Porter's Pass, Arthur's Pass and across the Crown Range and beyond into Queenstown.

One question loomed large in my mind: If I can cycle around one country, how far could I take this? Would it be crazy to cycle around the world?

9
RUN FATBOY RUN

Halloween bank holiday Monday in Dublin City, and for once the traffic chaos of the marathon road closures was going to work in my favour, as I got to run safely on the traffic-free roads of the capital city. My final long slow run two weeks earlier had picked up the marathon route at Heuston Station and I stuck as close to the route as I could until I reached Ranelagh. Instead of taking a right turn towards UCD and Clonskeagh, I kept going straight back towards my apartment in Sandymount.

I was a little concerned that I'd only managed seventeen miles in training, ideally I'd have gotten to at least twenty one, but my preparation had been thrown by the cycling trip to New Zealand only returning to Ireland and my training programme three weeks out from the main event.

My friend Liam had agreed to do the marathon with me. He'd been consistently quicker than me in training and we had expected something similar from him this time around, too. However an injury picked up before the race threatened to sideline him completely.

In the end he decided that he'd do the race but stick to my pace for as long as he could to support me. It turned out that the slower pace kept his injury from flaring up and when I eventually had to admit defeat, he was on hand to help me walk the final nine kilometres of the event.

A mixture of a walk and a shuffle continued while my shins felt as if someone was actually slicing through them with a sharp blade with each and every step I took towards the finish line.

Passing within half a kilometre of my apartment with five kilometres to go was particularly tough mentally. The worst was having the finish line in sight, only to find out a lap of Trinity College was required before crossing it.

Finally, Liam and I managed to reach the finish line together. The last hundred metres of that event will probably go down as one of the best feelings in my life. Over six and a half hours after the start of the race, I had completed the impossible. The marathon had been beaten.

I hadn't set the world alight and the Olympic hopefuls certainly wouldn't be worried about me stealing their spot on the team, but I had beaten the only competitor who I'd actually been battling against the entire time: myself.

10

50 FIRST DATES

My decision to go on 50 blind dates over the year may have been the one thing that kept me honest. I did meet 50 lovely ladies that year. Well 49 lovely ladies and a bloke.

My man-date was with Andy when JP, a mutual friend, thought it would be hilarious as a prank. To be fair to JP, he made amends by setting me up on another date immediately afterwards.

There were some second dates and even some third and fourth encounters, but the ones who interested me weren't interested back and vice versa.

I think it's important that I lay out the rules surrounding this aspect of my challenges.

Firstly, I was actually trying to meet a potential girlfriend. It wasn't about hitting a certain target number or getting a different girl every week. If the girl of my dreams had appeared on my second, third or whatever date, I would have closed that book and marked the adventure a success.

Secondly, every girl had to know exactly what I was doing. If she wasn't comfortable with that then we wouldn't even be having a first date. Total honesty from the start was the only way forward.

The third rule was that I couldn't even plan my date with the next girl until I was certain I had already had my last date with the current girl. There would be no dating a number of girls at the same time on this particular project.

Finally, and perhaps most importantly, no matter how well I hit it off with someone, there would be no question of hitting a home run on a first date. Telling the girls this in advance had been a good plan, as they were more relaxed, and no awkward sexual tension came into play throughout the dates. The established boundaries certainly made for more enjoyable evenings, the girls were comfortable and it certainly led to more offers of second dates.

11
THE ART OF THE DEAL

It was a phone call I received in the final week, just days after completing the Dublin City Marathon that would finally bring results on the employment front.

On the other end was Aidan, from a company called GrabOne, a daily deals website owned by the Irish Independent, similar to RateMyArea, with whom I'd been involved earlier in the year.

After reintroducing himself, he started by asking a few questions.

"Did you work for Swim Ireland?" he asked.

"No, although I was next door for a few years," I replied.

"Close enough. Did you work for RateMyArea?" Aidan asked.

"Yeah, earlier in the year for a short while," I replied.

I paused. I was wondering where this was going and I expressed my surprise at the line of conversation. He explained his real reason for calling.

"I'm friends with Trish, she worked in Swim Ireland beside

you, and your name came up in conversation the other day about all the challenges you've done this year," he said.

Trish had been one of the people who joined me for the initial duathlon ten months earlier to kick start my year.

"As you know, I'm National Sales Manager with GrabOne, would you be free for a coffee and a chat?" he asked.

Twenty four hours later I was sitting in front of Aidan, discussing whether I might be interested in working for GrabOne. I'm not going to lie: the job, the atmosphere and the financial package on the table were all very attractive.

Within a few minutes of leaving the building Aidan called me and asked me to come back for a formal interview and presentation with two of his colleagues. The meeting happened the following week and I suspected it had gone well.

Within an hour I received an email from Ruairi, the CEO of GrabOne, offering me a temporary position with a view to a more permanent position in January. While I was interested in the role, the monetary offer was much lower than expected. I asked for another meeting with him.

The following afternoon, I sat opposite Ruairi and explained that I while I was interested in principle, I wouldn't be accepting his offer unless the money on the table was doubled at a minimum. I started work there the day before my Challenge Ten project was due to finish.

I would be starting my new job, which I had been head hunted for, with a salary, benefits and a respect that dwarfed the role I'd left at the start of the year.

Things couldn't have gone any better for me. I'd closed my first deal on day one, and had been moved from a temporary contract to a full time contract after five days on the job.

12
CHARIOTS
OF FIRE

At the end of the thirteen months I'd given myself to complete the Challenge Ten, the guy in the mirror was no longer someone I wanted to get as far away from as possible. I had become someone who was much more confident in my own skin, happier in my own company and surrounded by a smaller, but much closer bunch of friends and family.

The thoughts that had been constant in my head just a year earlier were no more. I no longer spent all day thinking about how my life wasn't worth living and whether people would be better off without me.

I had bad days, of course, but on the whole I was a different person from the person who had written the list which I had just spent a year crossing items off.

Sharing my innermost thoughts and fears with others had brought me to a point where I knew that I had people around me who loved and supported me, they had been there always, I just couldn't see that at the time.

* * *

I planned my next steps over the next eighteen months. It was obvious to me I had an ambition to be competitive in sports. Months of finishing runs and swims and being far closer to the wooden spoon than the podium saw me developing more creativity in the kinds of events I might enter. I knew my total lack of running and swimming ability were never going to allow me to be competitive on the road or in the water, but on a bicycle I was passing people for fun in any triathlon or duathlon in which I competed.

That being said, I'd never entered a bicycle race, I really didn't have a reference by which to judge myself. I decided I needed to find a really long bicycle race where it wouldn't just fall to pace in the saddle. I needed to find a race that was longer than anything I knew about; a race that would allow for plenty of mishaps and misfortune that might occur and by a minor miracle leave me in the running for a place on the podium.

I had a picture of the tortoise and the hare racing, except on bicycles. That led me to doing what everyone does when they want to research something. I Googled "World's longest bike race," and my computer screen spat out 'The World Cycle Race'.

When I scratched at the surface, I found the race was just a few weeks away from the start of its first edition in London. I was going to have to wait until the next time the event would be run. I followed the race as Mike Hall, Richard Dunnett and Simon Hutchinson made their way around the planet and finished the race in that order. Of the eleven competitors, only three had completed the ordeal. This looked like my kind of event: it was so long and difficult that it didn't just take speed into consideration, so my sheer persistence and being too stubborn to quit might be enough to compete.

13
THE DAY THE EARTH STOOD STILL

Life went on largely as planned over the coming months. Work followed work, day after day, and life had become slightly tedious and boring again. I'd slipped back into some old habits. I'd returned to the world of living from pay cheque to pay cheque, keeping up with the Joneses.

I longed to return to my days of adventure, sport and trying new things. I went to London for the weekend in September 2012 to watch Ireland try and collect some silverware at the Paralympic Games. I'd managed to get my hands on two tickets and even found myself a date for the evening's action.

Gemma, one of my original fifty dates, was living in London, and proved to be great company for the evening's events. Three Irish gold medals, the most successful haul ever by an Irish team at a major sports event on a single day, were eclipsed by my date's allegiances to three nationalities, namely Britian, South Africa and New Zealand, which combined to trounce Ireland's total. I didn't care. I was enjoying her company too much to even notice.

* * *

Six months later, sitting in my kitchen in Sandymount, I heard voices from the radio talk about suicide and cycling. The voice spoke about a nationwide cycle to promote a positive message about mental health and suicide prevention using cycling as the vehicle to spread that message. They had left the campus of the national broadcaster, RTE, that morning but I quickly found the website they had mentioned: Cycle Against Suicide.

I marked the last three days, when the event would be travelling from County Leitrim, my home, to Dublin, where I'd gone to University and since had spent nearly my entire adult life. I booked my spot.

A week later, my sister dropped me the short distance to Manorhamilton in North Leitrim where I joined a large group of orange-clad cyclists all bound for Cavan. As we made our way along the byways of Leitrim, I fell in beside total strangers and by the time we got separated a few minutes later we were on first name terms. There was a very strange vibe in this group, but good strange. It was very different to anything I'd experienced before, although I couldn't quite put my finger on why.

At our first stop in Belturbet, we were practically force-fed biscuits, sandwiches and tea by the fantastic teachers in the school. I made my way into the larger classroom where a small presentation space had been set aside amongst the small chairs that were all occupied around the room. Three of us grabbed a space on the floor and started listening to the speakers.

Rob Carley talked about losing his wife Jean, his childhood sweetheart, dealing with his own demons, and finding love again. Nigel offered practical advice on dealing with depression and identifying it in others around you. Radio Presenter Colm Hayes offered his experience dealing with mental health issues and how that had materialised in his world.

It was all tied up by Niall Breslin, known to most Irish people as Bressie, a former professional athlete, front man of Irish band The Blizzards and most recently a judge on The Voice of Ireland.

A mere mention of his name sent the girls into raptures, with squeals loud enough to raise the roof. Niall shared stories about how he had dealt poorly with his anxiety and mental health issues over the years until recently when he had admitted he had a problem and sought out the help that was needed to treat his issues.

Sitting on the cold floor in Belturbet, surrounded by students and cyclists, everyone wearing orange, I resolved that I was going to do everything I could to share this message as far, wide and as loud as I could possible manage. An idea was already forming.

14

FIELD OF DREAMS

I waited for the dust to settle and after a few weeks I wrote an email to Cycle Against Suicide, outlining my ambition to cycle around the world and asking whether I could do it to raise awareness for the message they promoted along the way. I sat down with Maghnus Collins, their CEO, a week or so later and I outlined my plans for the second edition of the World Cycle Race. He couldn't have been more supportive.

Now that I had actually told someone else my plans it felt more real. Things started picking up a pace over the summer of 2013. I reached out to a few friends who had undertaken major physical events of their own in recent years for advice.

Gerry Duffy, who'd completed not only 32 marathons in 32 days, but followed that up by winning a race over 10 iron distance triathlons in 10 consecutive days in the summer of 2011 was my first mentor as I planned my trip. He would become one of my main mental supports as I trained for my ride.

Simon Hutchinson, the Irish man who'd finished third the

previous time around, was equally supportive. Now based in Vancouver, we had conversations over Skype and Facebook where he answered my never-ending flood of questions about his route, equipment, training regime, nutrition and his mental state as he progressed through the ride.

I attempted to contact most of the nine individuals who had previously completed the ride and managed to get advice from most of them. The group, especially Simon, Mike Hall, Vin Cox and Juliana Buhring were generous with their time and supportive with their expertise. Speaking to each of them made the race, which had seemed so ridiculous at times, now look like it was achievable.

To focus on the physical challenge, I quit my job. I was now out of work, and without bike racing experience or equipment suitable for the challenge ahead. I hadn't even told my parents.

I applied for a funding programme for sports projects which benefited communities and community groups. The first stage was to seek votes from the public, and my mother finally discovered my plans when my cousin saw it on Facebook and showed it to her.

A few days later my mum and dad came to visit me in Dublin on some other pretext, but I'd been warned by my cousin ahead of time that they were there to talk me out of the World Cycle Race. When I explained what I wanted to do, they were, to put it mildly, unenthusiastic.

Initially, my mother was not supportive in the slightest. Her final comment on the matter was as you would expect from most Irish mothers "When you don't get the funding for this madness, you have to settle down, grow up and get a proper job".

I was already pretty certain that I wouldn't be able to get the funding I'd applied for, but by the end of the lengthy online voting campaign, I'd managed to get enough support and attention to reach the top ten projects but it wasn't enough to convince the judges.

I was gutted, and I was back to square one: without funding and still, despite my training, grossly underprepared for the scale of the race. I now had even less time to rectify both of those problems.

I may not have got the funding, but the whole experience led to a chain of events that got me a step closer to my goal, and before I knew it I was being trained by coaches Conor Clifford, Daithi McCabe, Kevin Croke and Cliodhna O'Connor at the National Athlete Development Academy. I was given the once-over with a functional movement screen, and they set me a strength and conditioning programme focusing on building the joints that would be taking the majority of the impact on the bike: my ankles, knees, hips and lower back.

Seán Kinane took me through a VO2 max test on the bike to measure my ability to use oxygen efficiently. Meanwhile, Leinster Rugby's nutritionist Daniel Davey took a look at my dietary intake and laid out a plan for what I should be consuming to fuel my body for the challenge ahead.

2008 & 2012 Olympian Colin Griffin, owner of Altitude Centre Ireland, joined me in the gym one morning a week to get me acclimatised to the trials of exercising at higher altitude levels. The benefits of the training is being not only about replicating the experience I would have crossing the Rocky Mountain Range in the American leg of the journey, but improving my immune system, my circulation and my general fitness levels.

Around this time, I got a phone call from my mother asking if I was in my apartment in Dublin. She and my dad were on the way back from a funeral of an in-law relative at the other end of the country and they wanted a chat. I wasn't really looking forward to it, I was still annoyed about the response I had gotten the last time we spoke, but an hour or so later they arrived at the door. As it turned out, the table conversation after the funeral had almost entirely consisted of one topic: me.

A distant in-law had seen my campaign on social media, and he was enthused by how fantastic it looked and how vital the message was that I was trying to spread. Over the course of their hour-long visit, my parents finally got to understand why I wanted to do this. It wasn't about me going for a cycle holiday, it was about trying to set an example of what was possible. My goal was to inspire people, to suggest that regardless of the situation you were in right now, anyone can do something that most people considered amazing. Even if the starting point was one of the darkest places imaginable. My parents hugged me and told me they would move heaven and earth to make sure I got to complete this cycle. They had just become my biggest supporters.

Within a matter of weeks after starting NADA's training regime, I could barely recognise myself. I was feeling stronger on the bike and losing so much weight that I was really beginning to believe that I might be able not only to start the World Cycle Race, but also to finish it.

The training was a test of character that I hadn't been subjected to before. Each time I woke up at four thirty to the sound of the rain on the roof and windows, I knew I not only had the commute to the gym but also the actual session itself ahead of me. Nearly every time I woke, I considered just rolling over and going back to sleep. Somewhere, though, I knew that if I made the decision to not go, even once, I'd never get myself into a condition to compete.

I needed to build up to cycling 700 km a week as part of my training, which didn't come easily.

At weekends, I would cycle the 170 kms from Dublin to Leitrim and back. I started by completing half of the journey by train to Mullingar and cycle the 80 kms home, but eventually I was clearing the entire 170 km distance unaided.

My first attempt at the complete distance was a disaster. My friend Louise was joining me from Enfield and I woke up nearly an hour late. I grabbed the bag I'd packed the night before and was out the door before I'd even woken up. Just outside Maynooth, I picked up a puncture and managed to change the tube myself, but my small pump wasn't really doing the job. I found myself in a bike shop in nearby Kilcock watching the guy change my flat. This was going to be something I needed to look at learning how to do better. By the time I met Louise in Enfield, she wasn't too impressed with me and my troubles.

We had barely passed Mullingar when my left pedal started to wobble. Then, it fell off the bike whilst still clipped into the bottom of my cycle shoe. Things weren't looking good. Louise, who'd been riding just ahead of me, looped back and we inspected the damage.

After an aborted attempt to cycle with just one foot, I ended up walking the bike to the top of the hill and rolling down the other side into the petrol station at Ballinalack. My makeshift repair job lasted only a few kilometres before I finally admitted defeat just after Edgeworthstown and called for a ride to my parents'. I was going to have to work out a better disaster recovery plan.

15
THE COLOUR
OF MONEY

I'd approached the editor of the Irish Independent's FIT Magazine about getting some exposure for the cycle in the magazine through the trip. I was hoping that the added exposure might help in the hunt for sponsors. The editor, Vicki, asked me to send in a piece for the following week's edition about my story in relation to positive mental health and that we'd gauge what the reaction was.

After a few weeks of chasing her about a decision she finally replied to my email saying she didn't have a budget to consider doing something on a weekly basis. I'd never asked for money, I hadn't even really thought about it.

She asked me to call in the following day, and I struggled to hold my composure as I was offered a weekly column and payment beyond what I could have hoped for..

A clothing supplier, Spin11, came on board to sponsor specially designed cycling gear, and they even produced a replica version of the jersey they gave me as a potential perk for the crowdfunding campaign too. I knew I needed more money to make the World Cycle Race a reality, but I didn't want to be going around cap in hand asking for donations. The crowdfunding campaign would produce half of my entire budget. The other half came from the writing gig, a tax rebate I was due, a small gift from my grandmother, some donations from friends and family and two fundraising raffles on my send-off nights in Leitrim and Dublin.

I was ready to go.

January and February were spent poring over maps, budgets and bike equipment, figuring out which set of lights to take with me, which pedals and shoes to equip myself with, what saddle might help the most with the pain I was anticipating to deal with over the coming months. Although local and national press, radio and TV took some interest, I honestly don't think anyone, even the people who were helping me, thought I had a chance in hell of completing the course. To be honest, I wasn't entirely sure myself.

One incident in training that springs to mind was on one long Sunday spin back to Dublin, a lone rider on a training spin ghosted by me as if I was stopped. I started to question the sanity of what I was doing. I'd never even taken part in a bike race before, not even an informal one. I'd no pedigree in bikes and here I was thinking of taking on the longest endurance sporting event in the world, with the hope of actually winning it, and maybe even breaking a world record in the process. I'd done the maths, it was possible. It was highly unlikely, but it was possible.

When I wrote my column for FIT Magazine that week, I was comparing myself to the tortoise in the classic Aesop's fable about his race with the hare. I was being realistic about my chances. In total, seven competitors had entered the race: Rolland from France, Nathan from the USA, Prasad from India, me from Ireland, Lee and Jason from the United Kingdom and a German girl, Fran. I was most definitely ranking myself absolutely last in terms of experience, speed and fitness levels. It was going to have to be a real-life version of the fable.

To snatch a podium place, I was banking on other aspects of the ride to affect the other competitors worse than they would affect me. I might be able to take advantage of the length, the terrain, the equipment, the restrictive nature of rules of the race, and even the financial and visa considerations to beat a few of the competitors.

I must have read the rules of the race multiple times every day. Adopted from those set by Guinness World Records and recognised by the entire long distance cycle racing community, some of the rules were quite obvious. Having to finish your ride at the exact point where you started, wearing a helmet at all times and travelling in a single uninterrupted line in a single direction.

Travel, including flights and ferries, had to total at least 40,075km, the length of the equator. 29,000km of which had to be in the saddle.

Each person's route had to pass through two cities that were antipodal. That meant on the exact opposite side of the globe. I planned two such set of cities for my route, Wellington, NZ mirrored Madrid, and Hamilton, NZ mapped onto Cordoba. No private transport was to be used. Only scheduled and ticketed public transport was permitted, and then only in the face of an ocean, an impassable object, or a country which wasn't safe.

With my every free moment I was consuming knowledge about the challenge I had ahead of me, making Skype calls to previous finishers, and reading books like *The Man Who Cycled the World* by Mark Beaumont, who smashed the original record back in 2008. The World Cycle Race had taken over my life.

My Irish pride wouldn't let the defining moment of my life start and end in London. The start of the race, in Greenwich, wasn't going to be my personal start or end point. I didn't have control over the race, so I decided to start and end my cycle journey at my home in Leitrim Village and to make my way to and from Greenwich from there.

Sara and Louise had agreed to come as my backup team for the event. Sara, an accomplished photographer and videographer, would be looking after the social media and blogging aspects of the trip. Louise, a globe-trotting fitness and nutrition geek with a qualification in massage therapy and plenty of experience around bikes, would be driving the support vehicle and overseeing the logistics for the trip. I'd worked with both of them before on various projects and I picked them for their experience and expertise.

As the days to the race ticked down, I was getting excited about the challenge ahead. I was invited to speak in my old school, Sligo Grammar School, about my plans for the race and just days before the race started I found myself at the top of my old classroom with the familiar faces of my school teachers looking up at me as I spoke about my experience with mental health and the battle I was facing into in the weeks and months ahead.

Standing in front of those students, I knew I couldn't let myself down with this challenge. Seeing the faces of my former school teachers, such influences in my teenage years, it really hit home that I was about to set off on a fantastic adventure, but that at some level, each of these people would be joining me along the way.

SEND OFF

22nd February - 23rd February, 2014

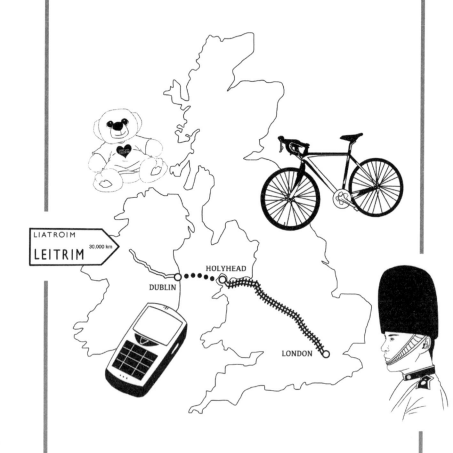

Distance: 166km

Elevation: 573 metres

16

WITH A LITTLE
HELP FROM
MY FRIENDS

I didn't get any sleep that Friday night and I was the first one out of bed in my parent's house. The following morning it was unusually dry and relatively warm for late February in North West Ireland.

I felt nervous and excited. I had no real expectation or knowledge of what was waiting ahead of me. The reality that it would be many months and 30,000 kms in the saddle before I'd return to see my family, friends and neighbours again hadn't yet sunk in at that point.

Sara was up soon after I started pottering around. We ate a full Irish breakfast and discussed plans for the day. Just before nine o'clock I pushed my new best friend, my bike, through the back door, swung my leg over the cross bar, and set off.

The meeting point for the day was the community centre in the village. There were three people in the car park pulling bike frames and wheels out of cars. I had been expecting a dozen or so local riders from the local cycling and triathlon clubs to join me for the first few kilometres of the day and I was pleased to see activity but I was worried that there wouldn't be as much support as I'd hoped for.

About two minutes before the allotted time a group of cyclists from the local cycling club arrived, and they were swiftly followed by another group from the triathlon club and finally a social cycle group from nearby Battlebridge.

The Cycle Against Suicide family were well represented by Niall, Kenneth and Colm. My disappointment evaporated as the car park was now full with bikes and lycra-clad cyclists. Even my sisters joined me for the start.

The first spin into the local bike shop, Trailblazers, in Carrick on Shannon, passed in something of a blur. The nervous excitement had been amplified by the amazing number of people who had come out to say 'goodbye' and 'good luck'. This was now real, the concept which I had first formulated, sitting on the floor of that classroom in Belturbet during the first Cycle Against Suicide wasn't just an idea anymore. It had grown legs, pedals and wheels, and the clock was running.

Sunday morning saw eleven souls leave Tri & Run, a bicycle and triathlon shop in Mullingar. We collected some more bodies through Kinnegad, Enfield and Maynooth until we grew into a group of almost a hundred cyclists entering Dublin along the quays of the River Liffey. We finished up in Sandymount in Dublin, to have a send-off celebration in my local pub, Mulligan's of Sandymount. The hundred or so people who gathered to say farewell that evening in Dublin represented nearly all strands of my life in Dublin. College, work, friends, various sports teams and my Cycle Against Suicide family were all represented. I couldn't have asked for a better send off.

17
LONDON CALLING

The day prior to the start saw a race briefing and a press launch with the race organisers, The League of Adventurists International, the people responsible for such craziness as the 'Mongol Rally', a car race between London and Ulaanbaatar, and a 3,500km drive in a tuc-tuc through India known as the 'Rickshaw Run'.

Dan and Joolz from the Adventurists met Lee, Fran and myself along with a few others involved behind the scenes to run through the rules of the race, the plan for tomorrow's race start and the other details we would each need to know as the race progressed. There was no sign of the fourth competitor, Jason, at the press launch, but he was expected to join us at the start line the following day, while the final remaining competitor, Prasad, was starting on the same day in Bangkok, as the sole participant heading in a westerly direction. We were informed that the other two competitors, Nathan and Rolland, were no longer participating in the event, leaving just five competitors. My tortoise theory had already claimed two victims.

* * *

We each signed an entry form stating we'd read the rules and were taking responsibility for our own participation in the race, absolving the race organisers of blame if we were to get seriously injured or even killed. This kind of form is pretty standard at every outdoor activity centre in the world, but this was the first time I signed the form thinking there was a possibility that it may actually be required in this instance.

From there we walked around the corner to the actual press launch of the race, it was to be held in the Brooks store in central London. Brooks, a saddle and bike bag manufacturer, were the sponsors of the race, and I'd selected a saddle from their range to be an integral part of my equipment for the ride. After a while spent mingling with the assembled audience and journalists, the master of ceremonies Buddy Munro introduced the three riders who were starting from Greenwich the following day. Fran, Lee and I were all quizzed on our preparations, plans and strategies to get us around the world in one piece.

Tommy Moran, our host at the Crown Moran Hotel in London, kindly invited all three of us to the ICAP Annual Dinner which was to be held in the Inner Temple along the north bank of the Thames in central London. The night was being run to raise funds for a mental health service to the Irish community in London.

It was a great evening's entertainment, and when the master of ceremonies introduced me to the room and explained to the large group present what I was to face the following morning, I was surprised and humbled by the reaction. The evening was pretty phenomenal, as the great and good of the Irish community in London approached me to wish me well on my journey.

* * *

Marble Arch was a sea of blue t-shirts and World Cycle Race flags the next morning as I cycled to the meeting point.

There was still no sign of Jason when Lee, Fran and I lined up beside 2012 race winner Mike Hall and special guest Joff Summerfield, who had cycled around the world on his penny farthing. I set off with a motley crew of cyclists to take over the streets of London and make the journey to the official race start line in Greenwich.

Sixty cyclists took to the streets to join us on our way past Buckingham Palace, Trafalgar Square, Westminster Abbey, Big Ben & the Houses of Parliament, The River Thames, The Tower of London and across Tower Bridge before ending up at the Cutty Sark and entering Greenwich Park.

It was going up the steep hill from the village side of the park that I first questioned whether I might have made a mistake entering the race. I was trying to cover up my puffing and panting going up the hill and each of the other cyclists in the group were simply flying by me. This wasn't even a mountain.

At the top of the climb, the Royal Observatory came into view, and the start line of the race was now a reality.

Jason, the fourth rider, never appeared, and we set off about twenty minutes later than scheduled. I was beside Lee and Fran on the start line as the Master of Ceremonies, Buddy Munro, was talking to the audience getting them prepped for a rousing send off when I realised I had no idea which direction Dover was. I knew where it was on a map, but in all the excitement I hadn't remembered to bring the directions or a route from Greenwich to Dover. The global route I'd so painstakingly devised remained exactly where I'd left it: on my laptop.

EUROPE

1st March - 4th April, 2014

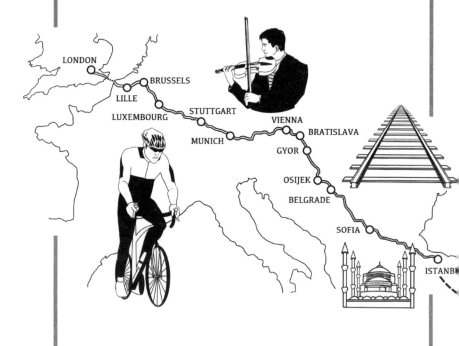

LONDON

BRUSSELS

LILLE

LUXEMBOURG

STUTTGART

MUNICH

VIENNA

BRATISLAVA

GYOR

OSIJEK

BELGRADE

SOFIA

ISTANB

Distance: 3,962km
Elevation: 29,700 metres

18
THE GREAT RACE

With about a hundred people at the start line I figured it was way too late to give the game away and expose myself as an imposter who had no place being at the start of a bike race around the planet. I jokingly asked out loud "Which way to Dover?" which elicited a rumble of laughter from the crowd but no actual answer. I looked to my right and left. it appeared as if I was in good company. Fran didn't have a clue which direction we were going either, and Lee was frantically fiddling with his GPS device to establish his route.

I decided my best course of action would be to follow them until we got far enough out of the city that the road signs would guide me to the ferry terminal and I would get an opportunity to regroup there and set out my plan of attack on mainland Europe. The avenue out of the park was a straight line, but the less than amazing GPS services that Fran and Lee were employing, albeit better for the moment than my non-existent one, told them to turn to the left. I followed their lead. It was mildly embarrassing to complete the other two sides of the triangle and re-join the main channel through the park while the crowd of people still watching us from the start line at the Observatory.

The three of us took a left turn out of the park before Lee started to pull away from me and Fran. I hadn't fully expected the race to actually start like a race from the off. In much the same way as an athlete doesn't sprint from the start line of a marathon, I naively expected us to more or less all be together until we reached the ferry in Dover.

Lee had appeared a bit aloof and distant coming into the event, my attempts to make contact through social media hadn't even been acknowledged. Fran, Prasad and I had been comparing notes on everything, including routes, equipment, strategy, different forms of accommodation. Lee had chosen to stay out of that discussion and had just got on with his own planning. It wasn't all that surprising when we lost him within a mile or two of leaving the park.

The A2, the main route to Dover, was a dual carriageway and one sign indicated that bikes weren't allowed on the route. After checking the route plan on Google Maps, I decided to take my chances rather than getting caught in a maze of small roads and potentially missing the ferry.

I ploughed on towards Dover and for the first hour or so Fran was never further than a few hundred metres behind me on the road.

It was at that point of the ride when I realised I'd lost Fran. She wasn't tailing me anymore, my first reaction was to worry whether I'd taken a wrong turn but a quick check and I knew I was on the right path. I stopped for a quick snack at a petrol station near Sittingbourne after about sixty kilometres and when she hadn't arrived I figured she'd either stopped elsewhere, had a mechanical problem, or taken a different, quieter route.

Getting back on the road I was really happy with the progress I was making when about thirty kilometres outside of Dover I reached the bottom of a long drag which seemed to go on forever. Half way up the climb I was feeling a little tired and decided to stop for a moment and as I pulled into the side of the road a cyclist appeared just behind me. It was Kristoff Allegaert, the Transcontinental Race Champion, who had decided to cycle over from Belgium to London for the day simply to be at the start of the race. He was now on the return journey home.

Kristoff slowed to ensure I was okay and left me standing at the side of the road with the parting words "Don't stop! Always keep moving!" Within a minute I was back on the bike and pounding the pedals to get back up the hill. Try as I might, I just couldn't keep Kristoff in my sights and within a few kilometres he had left me in his dust.

The girls appeared in the support car as I reached the outskirts of Dover, a friend of Sara's had offered to drive them to Dover. I had a rental car booked in Calais that would cover our adventures on mainland Europe.

I spotted them parked at the terminal of the ferry on my descent from the top of the white cliffs to the sea level town. Despite being slightly later than expected, I managed to get tickets for the ferry I had planned to ride, and we joined our respective queues to board. The two girls, now carless, went with the rest of the foot passengers while I cycled to the water's edge and joined the other traffic preparing to board. I slept through most of the ferry and on arriving in Dover I disembarked with Kristoff and the other vehicles on the ferry while the girls made their way through the foot passenger route.

19
LOST IN LUXEMBOURG

I was the first rider in the race to make landfall on the other side of the channel. With directions from Kristoff I rode my bike to the terminal building to find the two girls standing outside the car rental office, which was closed and, by all indications, wouldn't be open again until Monday.

I checked the booking and realised I'd mistakenly booked the car from ten in the morning, and not the evening, when we actually arrived, so I rang the rental company, but quickly realised I didn't speak French well enough to explain the situation.

Louise, who had much a stronger grasp of the language, established that the number was just for emergencies and not for pickups. We weren't going to be able to get our wheels until Monday morning at the earliest.

We found the girls a place to stay, and I continued on alone through the darkness, on a road heading south-east, away from the English Channel and towards the city of Lille. Arques was sixty kilometres from Calais, and I really didn't want to waste the money I'd paid for my accommodation there.

I ended up hitting a pothole at pretty decent speed in the darkness and burst a tube, which forced me to change my front tube on the side of the road in the dark. It was after 1 AM when I reached the motel. I dried myself off after my shower and I slept until day break when I woke up, put on my lycra, and set off on the road.

At the top of the road out of the estate I reached my first roundabout. I was half way around the roundabout when a car entered from the opposite direction. A long blast of the horn from the irate driver woke me from the slight daze I was in, and I quickly realised I'd been on the left hand side of the road since leaving the hotel. I quickly turned myself and the bike around and exited the roundabout in the correct direction. I was sure confusing which side of the road to be wasn't the only issue I was going to have as I moved between countries and cultures on this trip.

I spent most of the afternoon on a bike and footpath along the canal, crossing into north Belgium at some point in the early evening. I stopped at a roadside diner which was absolutely jammed with locals. They looked surprised when I said I was aiming to make it to Brussels that evening. It was only two hours to sundown, but the hostel I'd booked in Brussels lay seventy kilometres south of the cafe.

By nightfall I was running on empty. I had no spare tubes remaining. I rolled into the town of Aalst just as their local music festival parade was starting. My route through the town was completely blocked off, and as darkness fell I realised I hadn't charged my lights from the previous evening. With no lights and no spare tubes, I had no option but to find local accommodation in the town and wait until the sun was up the following day. An early start the following day saw me make the remaining 40km into Brussels knowing that the girls would be picking up the rental car that morning and would hopefully have caught up with me by lunch time somewhere south of Brussels. I took a route straight through the Belgian capital, stopping in a few places to take in the beautiful surroundings. My front tyre was a little flat so I went looking for a bike shop as I left the city. I found a place on Google on the way out of town towards the south but it was closed when I got there. It turns out most bike shops in Western Europe are closed on Mondays.

I found a great bike path along the side of the motorway and was flying along, knowing the girls were en route with my clothes, more spare tubes, and all my power cables. Then, disaster struck with another flat tyre, this time thanks to a small bunch of debris scattered in the mouth of a tunnel under the motorway. I now had no tubes left, I was about four kilometres south of Brussels and a quick online search told me there was a bike shop that might actually be open, back in the city, just a few kilometres away.

I ended up hiking between the fabulous residences scattered across the hills of south Brussels for the next hour, pushing the bike with its single inflated tyre. When I walked through the door of the bike shop, I almost cried with happiness. I stocked up with three more tubes and replaced my lights with a much better set. I also decided to bite the bullet and bought a Garmin Edge 800 GPS device, I'd been putting it off beforehand, but now I realised I'd never make it to Germany without a proper navigation tool.

Once the bike was mobile again I cycled back to the point I'd already reached before turning on the SPOT tracker, and when two hours later I had stopped at a petrol station, another rider came into the shop after me. We got chatting and Pierre, who had almost perfect English, was enthralled to hear about my challenge. We rode together until Pierre suggested a better route. He brought me through a warren of roads via his own home back to the main road having avoided most of the busiest portions of the highway.

I reached the town of Namur and waited for the girls. I was about to charge my phone to contact them when they suddenly appeared outside the restaurant window and we went searching for a place to stay. The cheapest option for all three of us was called Chateau de la Poste, twenty kilometres further south. What the internet site didn't tell us was that the twenty kilometres travel distance was uphill.

About five kilometres outside of the town the road along the river turned to the left and up into the hills we went. I felt like the ride up the hill in the dark would never end, but eventually I found myself guided into a massive estate with a magnificent old country house fit for royalty at the top of the mountain overlooking the valley below. The view from the room the following morning was nothing short of spectacular. In what was to prove somewhat of a regular occurrence on the trip, the cheapest available place online at the last minute was one of the nicer places to stay.

It was dark when I crossed into the smallest country in the European Union and I made my way around the capital city to avoid the worst of the traffic. My target was a motel on the south side of the city which the girls had found. Darkness had already set in when I reached the motel, and after fighting with the staff to bring my bike inside they finally allowed me to put it in their secure storage area downstairs.

A decent breakfast the following morning set me up for the day, when I found myself traversing some hills in the countryside along the Luxembourg / Germany border. My Garmin GPS device told me to take a right turn off the main road, the road suddenly turned into a muck track half way down the descent, I had to get off the bike and walk it down the remainder of the hill. When I reached the end I found a grass path through a farm. I figured the road would restart just around the next bend or over the next rise. I could see the road again at the other side of the field and, after checking out the map, realised that my choices were to walk through the farm paddocks or go back through the mud to the road at the top of the hill and spend nearly as long going around the other three sides of the farm on the road.

Hindsight would tell me that going around the farm was the better option. At the time, I decided to push the bike through the field, and when I reached the other side I discovered that the mud was caught in the wheels, brakes and chain of the bike. I had to stop at the next town to wash the bike in order to get it rolling again.

At the end of a long day I found myself running out of batteries. Both of my phones were on a low power level. I wasn't able to find the two girls as their phones were powered off and eventually my phone died. This was the main issue with the support car. The temptation was to leave everything that wasn't essential in the car to reduce the load on the bike. Things that weren't essential, like a phone charger.

I couldn't make contact or even find any internet access until late in the evening in a small town on the German / French border. I persuaded a pharmacist with very little English to allow me to use her computer to send a message to the girls. Once the message was sent, I returned to my perch in the small cafe across the road to wait. The girls arrived about an hour later and after charging my phones sufficiently I was back on the road.

That evening, approaching Karlsruhe, with the Rhine River off to the right hand side of the bike path was a very eerie experience. The headlights on the bike barely illuminated the road ten metres ahead of me and virtually nothing to the sides or behind me. Every single bird call or sound of an animal moving in the darkness brought with it some scary ideas of what might be lurking beyond my light.

20
CAST AWAY

It was a few days later, coming east out of Stuttgart, I decided to take the direct route over the mountains rather than the longer distance around the base of the hill. I was pushing along the top of the hill at a nice pace, enjoying the amazing view when a gunshot rang out through the valley below me. Almost immediately I heard another shot, and a quick volley of noise had me frantically looking for the source of the commotion. Rounding the next corner, I saw an army barracks below me, and the firing range to the rear of the compound was active. German soldiers were practising their marksmanship while trucks and jeeps rolled around the military compound. It seemed like a scene right out of a war movie, complete with the soundtrack. I tried not to draw any attention to myself, as I was not quite sure whether or not I was in a restricted area or not. A few minutes later, I saw a sign at the end of the road which, in German that I couldn't understand, was almost certainly telling me that my presence was forbidden past that point, so I turned around and started making my way back to the top of that climb again to try a different route.

As I approached the top of the climb I saw half a dozen soldiers, fully armed, standing in a group. I was more than a little intimidated by their presence, but I realised that I was going to have to stop and explain myself before they would let me through and continue my journey. Two of them took an interest in the cyclist approaching them from what should have been a dead end. The others were fixated on the hill behind me. Turning around I spotted a few tanks and dozens of soldiers running drills at the top of the hill. I explained my situation in my best broken German to the soldiers, and they let me pass.

Approaching Ulm, I took the lessons learned from Brussels and avoided the city centre, charting a route north of the city through the rolling hills. As the sun prepared to go down for the evening, I was still looking at fifty kilometres to my intended stopping point and some pretty big climbs ahead. I had been finding the constant climbing very tiring and now, with light fading and facing into the mountains, I was feeling completely shattered. The first portion of the climb is through a vineyard, and as I sat for a quick break at the summit and looked back down at the motorway in the valley below, I realised that I'd just climbed higher than any Irish road even goes. This gorgeous view prepared me for the next challenge of getting to Augsburg before calling it quits for the night.

Eight days into the race and despite my best efforts I'd just fallen short of Munich, a short fifty kilometre spin lay between me and the home of Bayern, beer and bratwurst. Fran had just withdrawn, because of injury, from the World Cycle Race and was already back in her home in Munich and had offered me a place to stay, I landed just after lunch while the support car landed a few hours later.

I'd been following Lee's effort and he was so far ahead I knew I wasn't going to be able to catch him. Even if I managed to finish the race faster than the current world record, I wasn't going to beat Lee. That meant that I didn't stand a chance of holding the record myself. The support car just wasn't working out either. I honestly felt that it was slowing me down at a substantial expense.

I needed to change my approach. I needed to go solo and carry everything myself if I was going to succeed in completing my circumnavigation. I knew Fran was already out of the race. Prasad was having some problems with visas and finances already, and as he was still in India I suspected he wasn't going to be able to sort either of the issues out in time to really challenge me in the race. It's too bad, but it seemed like my Irish passport made a world of difference in terms of access to other countries.

Fran helped me change my approach and we set about ordering the gear required to carry my luggage on the bike. Together we made a new plan to adapt to a solo circumnavigation in less than 48 hours, including paying for a bike service to correct the wheel issues which had been ongoing since hitting that pot hole in the dark on the very first night in France.

I ordered the rest of the supplies and equipment I needed and as I was preparing to go back on the road, I sat down with Louise and Sara and we discussed the situation together. We agreed that it wasn't working and that everyone would be better served by going our separate ways. Arrangements were made, and after one final day in Munich the girls boarded a flight back to Dublin. My sister, Ruth, came out to bring the rental car back to Calais, but first she offered to help me get as far as Vienna.

21
THE SOUND OF MUSIC

I convinced Fran to join me to Istanbul as her Achilles tendon was now doing much better than it had been a few days earlier. Her ankle injury flared up again two hours outside of Salzburg. A quick phone call to Ruth saw her picked up from our break stop at a petrol station, and I took to the road once again, solo.

I said goodbye to Fran the following morning as she jumped on a train back to Munich. Ruth and I went east towards Linz and Vienna and planned on following the Danube towards the eastern side of the continent. I found the most amazing place that morning.

A lake sitting in the valley below the northern end of the Alps took my breath away. I was forced to stop and just sit and stare at the sheer beauty as the different shades of blue blended into each other across the lake and the mountains, which were just visible through the slight fog. It looked like something out of a painting, except it was real and it was just in front of me.

It took all the willpower I had to get back on the bike and leave that scene behind me, but I had a feeling I'd be having that speechless moment more than once before I'd reach my final destination on this trip.

For Ruth, Vienna would be the end of the line. She was heading to Italy en route back to Calais, and I needed to head off on my own. We woke up in Tulln, about an hour outside of Vienna, and picked a spot just on the west side of the city. I got back on Velo Route 6 along the Danube river while Ruth moved ahead to meet me at the other end of it. As I cycled along the river, I was wondering if I was making the right decision. Maybe I should just jump in the car with her and go home? It would certainly be a lot easier.

My mind was busy, but I spotted a fully-laden bicycle ahead of me along the path, ridden by a man with a full beard. I quickly pulled alongside him and slowed down to his pace.

"Guten Tag," he said.

"Guten Tag," I replied, asking him, "*Sprechen Sie Englisch?*"

"Yes! I'm English."

My new friend David explained how he had set off a few weeks earlier from London and was planning on spending a year or two cycling around the world. He was bound for Athens, Greece on this particular leg of the journey. We chatted while we rolled along at a leisurely pace for the next five or six kilometres. It was my first time meeting a complete stranger who understood what I was actually going through and knew why I had set out to do what I was in the process of undertaking.

As I reached Klosterneuburg, where I was to meet Ruth for the final time, I said goodbye to David and he rolled on towards Vienna. I eventually found Ruth and we met in the train station car park. I spent a while repacking bags and leaving things behind me before one last hug and goodbye. I wasn't sure when I would next see a member of my family or even a familiar face but I knew that I had to keep going east.

22

ME, MYSELF & I

I was back on the road. The bike path through Vienna kept me headed along the banks of the Danube and after crossing to the north bank of the river in the Austrian capital I found myself in the National Park for the remainder of the day.

The massive waterway to my right glistened in the afternoon sun as I made my way along the bike path built on top of what appeared to be a flood levy. The route was pretty quiet, with little to no activity other than a few wild animals and the occasional park ranger driving on the road below the flood barrier. The weather took a turn for the worse as I got closer to the Slovakian border and eventually I got soaked in the heavy rain. I found a supermarket whose manager eventually allowed me to bring in my bags and bike and decamp in their main doorway until the rain lightened up a bit. About an hour after I had stopped I set off for Bratislava, I rode across the border.

Despite it being a Saturday night I found a hostel in the city centre and immediately I was directed to an Irish bar where the St. Patrick's Day celebrations were in full swing, even though the

Irish national holiday didn't fall for another three days. Ireland had just clinched the Six Nations championship in rugby that day, and a local Gaelic football team had taken over the bar after their own competition. Everything was green, white and gold and the revellers were downing pints of the black stuff as if it wouldn't be available the following day or ever again.

The following day I got up and left Slovakia, crossing the border into Hungary. This was my first serious change. Now I was dealing with a new currency, the Hungarian Lev, my first non-Euro or Sterling currency of the trip, and English speakers were becoming scarce, too. I found myself in Gyro on my first night, in an old converted monastery along the bank of the river. The building and the rooms were pretty spectacular inside.

My legs and lower back were a little tight, so I went in search of a massage. I found a place a ten minute walk up the street and managed to book an hour session despite not having a word of Hungarian and the girl on the other end having no English.

I arrived at the location. A girl answered the door and showed me to the room where after some pleasantries, cut short by a lack of a common language, I stripped down to my shorts and lay face down on the table, waiting for her to return.

It was amazing. After more than two weeks and nearly two thousand kilometres in the saddle, the massage was exactly what my legs and lower back needed as she worked her magic. It was when she didn't stop working her way up my legs that I became a little bit worried. Eventually her hand disappeared inside the leg of my shorts. As I turned around to say I wasn't looking for that kind of service I realised she was completely naked. I explained using basic sign language that I was only interested in a massage without any extras or happy endings. I managed to get the message across and although she remained distractingly naked for the rest of the session, there was no more funny business.

23
FREE
FALLING

You know when you're watching a movie and you can predict exactly what's going to happen next, you can recite exactly what the lead character is going to say next, what the next plot twist is going to be, and which of the kids being "chased" by the killer is actually the killer himself. It's that moment when you groan and say, "That's just too obvious, who actually wrote this? Sack the scriptwriter."

St. Patrick's Day on the shore of Lake Balaton will always be that scene in the movie of my life. Let me set the scene.

I'm cycling down a hill, listening to *Simple Things*, a charity album released in Ireland for suicide prevention, when the first strains of the adopted theme song for the Cycle Against Suicide campaign, "Forget Me Knots" starts pumping through my earphones.

The catchy beat gets my hands tapping on the handlebars while I'm belting out the lyrics "It's alright not to feel okay" at the top of my voice. I spot the bike path restarting in the park on the far side of the train tracks along the shore of the lake to my right and as I enter the gate and prepare to cross the tracks, the quiet section of the song starts.

"Some people just don't understand what it feels like to fall. So don't fall, So don't fall. So don't fall, So don't fall."

This is the point of the movie where, as the soundtrack builds, the lyrics are advising me specifically not to do something, and I do it anyway. My front wheel manages to find the only crack in the pavement wide enough to take the tyre. My front tyre drops into the gap, acts like an emergency brake, and stops dead. Momentum takes over, and I find myself catapulted over the handlebars towards the pavement below. With my ears connected to the phone on the dashboard and my feet clipped into the pedals, the bike has no choice but to follow me and eventually my bike and I become a crumpled mess on the tarmac, a combination of carbon fibre, flesh and lycra on the bike path along the lake shore.

Two of the mothers in the nearby playground come over to see if I'm ok. I manage to stand up but my legs and arms are shaking from the shock of it. There's a little bit of blood coming out of my elbow and my right knee has a throbbing pain but everything seems generally fine I think I should be able to continue.

After a couple of painful kilometres around the lake, I find a bench where I stop to take better stock of what has just happened. My hands and feet are still shaking. Try as I might I'm not able to control their movements. A drink, a quick bite and a few minutes rest and things return mostly back to normal. I can make out the city of Siofok on the other side of the lake, although it's a good two hour cycle around the tourist attraction, even longer now that my bike and my body are a little bruised and broken.

As the darkness sets in, I reach the guesthouse that I've booked for the evening. At this stage, I'm barely able to walk on my knee, and I'm beginning to get slightly worried about what might be ahead of me tomorrow. The family who run the guesthouse change my booking to a ground floor room with an accessible bathroom. After showering and changing, the leg feels better and I walk the short distance towards the old water tower which marks the town's centre..

After a good night's sleep it's not until the following morning before I realise I'm not going anywhere. I book in for a second night and take a little while to slowly walk around the town and check out one of Hungary's top tourism spots, climbed the water tower in the centre of the town and spent what felt like hours just watching the fountain beneath. The second day after my fall, my knee felt much better, and I decided to get back on the bike and continue. The first few miles were a little tight, but as my body warmed up, my knee started to feel better and I kept pedalling.

As I cycled across the border from Hungary into Croatia and neared Osijek, it was like stepping back in time. Life just seemed to have slowed down. On the secondary roads there was minimal traffic and what was there crept along at a snail's pace, including tiny tractors carrying loose crops, driven by veteran farmers who fulfilled virtually every stereotype I'd heard of.

Watching the distance to Osijek getting smaller with each passing sign post, I started to get that feeling of possibility back in my head. Four years earlier in that Croatian city, I'd been the head coach of St. Francis, a women's soccer team, who represented Ireland in the UEFA Women's Champions League, winning one and losing one game in the three fixture group we were 3-0 down after seventeen minutes to the local team in our final game.

By the end of the game a fantastic performance from an amazing group of girls had seen us win the game on a 5-3 score line.

I'm pretty sure no one outside the dressing room under that near-empty stand at half time in the encounter thought we had a hope of turning that game around.

Fast forward a few years, and I was in a similar scenario, thousands of kilometres behind the race leader with a busted knee. I'd been struggling to match what Lee was doing on a daily basis before my fall, and now I was unable to see how that might change. I just had to keep plugging away and hope that things outside my control would develop in my favour.

I finally reached the outskirts of Osijek and made my way along the river bank just north of the city. The downtown area came into view and my heart skipped a beat. This was it. I was back at the location of the greatest sporting achievement I'd been involved in. Back in 2010, I'd been seriously struggling mentally at the time and I didn't really enjoy that event. I'd been worrying about work, my body, and a million other things that were flying through my mind on a daily basis, trying to avoid every camera, every social engagement and encounter with anyone.

I decided I was going to spend the night in Osijek to revisit some of the locations from that trip and soak up some of the memories four years after the event. I cycled past the posh hotel we'd stayed at along the banks of the river, quickly making the decision that a lycra-clad cyclist probably wasn't on their desired guest list. I quickly found a McDonalds in the main shopping street and availed myself of the golden arches and their complementary Wi-Fi that would become a regular companion of mine for the entire trip, connecting me to the outside world.

After finding a place to stay, my next priority was to find a bike shop. My front wheel hadn't been running true since the crash and needed to be realigned. Google threw up a bike shop just down the road and I made my way there. The shop owner was indifferent to my plight, but one of the boys in the back took a real interest, and he took my bike, replaced some spokes and got the wheel sorted out in just a few minutes.

I had booked a room in a guesthouse just around the corner, but there wasn't much to see when I got there aside from a locked gate with a sign in Croatian. I could make out a phone number but the rest of the sign meant absolutely nothing to me. I called the number but a woman who answered spoke no English. The impromptu sign language which had served me so well wasn't proving very helpful over the phone. A passer-by stopped and offered help. After a quick conversation they told me to wait where I was and the land lady would come and get me. Fifteen minutes later, an elderly woman approached me and we established that she was the voice on the other end of the phone. She started walking away from me waving me to follow her. I wasn't sure what to do, given that the lack of street lights and the eerie, abandoned-looking streets seemed like something out of a cheap slasher flick. I was trying to remember how many movies there had been in the *Hostel* franchise and wondering if the news reports of my demise would be the inspiration for the next instalment.

I brushed aside the horror movie in my head and followed the old woman, but the bad mental images came back when she turned down a narrow laneway between two buildings, barely wide enough for a single person to get through. Thankfully, the sight of a large courtyard and signs for hotels and other accommodations tipped the scales in her favour, and I followed to find I had a small apartment all to myself. As soon as she left, I found myself in the shower cleaning the grime from my body after a hard day in the saddle.

The following morning I took a detour out of town to visit the stadium where our Champions League games had taken place four years earlier. There had been some extensive development around the stadium, but it was essentially unchanged. I thought back to the astounding second-half performance from a great group of girls. I knew that I needed to just keep pedalling through the World Cycle Race. I had a long way to go.

24

THE TOWERING INFERNO

The next thing I needed to do to finish the race was to get into Serbia. This wasn't my first time to visit Serbia, but this time, things were very different. My previous visits were with Irish teams for World University Games or Championships.

For these visits, we were picked up at the plane and whisked through immigration, customs and baggage claim before air conditioned cars brought us to our hotel or the event village. Each of my three previous visits to the Serbian capital was filled with free food and water and being treated as if we were the most important people on the planet.

This time around, I was alone, sweaty and cycling towards a border checkpoint. No other buildings were visible on the horizon, just a row of trucks waiting to clear the border. I cheekily cycled past all the trucks and found myself at the top of the queue in a few minutes.

I got the usual two or three questions about my reasons for entering the country. When I explained I was heading for Istanbul and eventually around the world, the border guard's eyes grew wide, but within seconds his mind was back on the job and he waved me through.

All the road signs and maps were now using both the Roman and Cyrillic alphabets which proved challenging on the road to Novi Sad.

On the approach to the city, I met Eva & Slobodan, who were both from Novi Sad. I asked them for advice on where I might stay in the town and they gave me directions to a youth hostel.

"Would a couch work?" Eva asked me.

"Absolutely!" I replied.

Eva offered me a place to stay in her apartment. I met her teenage son Tarján as I walked through the door but when she brought me into her sitting room, which would double as my bedroom for the evening, I saw an entire wall was given over to her trophies and medals.

The framed photos dotted throughout the impressive haul of silver trophies indicated a stellar cycling career. Turns out the many-times national champion had competed at numerous World Championships for Yugoslavia her in younger days.

Eva had to leave to teach an English class, so she left me chatting to Tarján for the evening. When she returned, we joined Slobodan and his girlfriend for an evening in town.

We had a bite to eat and then Slobodan brought us to a salsa dancing club. He and his girlfriend were highly accomplished dancers, but my legs were screaming at me from the day's ride and I was ready for bed.

After an hour or so of soaking up the atmosphere I was ready to hit the hay. Eva and I took the short stroll home and I was asleep within minutes of my head hitting the pillow.

* * *

Belgrade was my target for the following day. However my directions let me down as soon as I left Novi Sad. The only real drawback of using Google Maps on a phone is that it doesn't tell you about elevation heights. I found myself turning left off the main road facing into a ridiculously steep climb of over 13% gradient in places. A long day ahead just got that little bit longer.

It took a few hours to get up and over the hill, I knew I was going to have to face into the mountains at some point during the day. It turns out I took the hardest route to the summit of the range separating Novi Sad and Belgrade, but the half-hour descent on the other side did make up for the rough climb.

I stopped at a little shop in the village at the bottom of the mountain to refuel and restock my water bottles. The descent had put me back on target to reach the capital in time to catch the Partizan Belgrade football game I'd had my eye on for a few days.

I reached the city and took a nostalgic tour around the old neighbourhood where we had stayed during the 2009 World University Games, including the building in which Team Ireland had been housed for that event.

During a fire evacuation, Ryan Coulter and I ran into the burning building to search for John Dooley, an Athletics coach asleep inside, as smoke billowed out of the windows from the seventh floor window immediately next door to his bedroom window. After waking John, the three of us got out of the building without incident.

I found a bed in a hostel near the city centre. When I reached the reception there was one guy about my age working in the place. He was very excited about my journey and was full of questions. He moved me from the dorm that I should have been in to give me my own space. Once we'd secured my bike on a private balcony and I showered, he practically demanded I go to the football game, but I had to do my laundry. He took my bag off me, telling me he'd take care of it, and sent me packing. I jumped in a taxi and within a few minutes I was handing over the sum of 250 Serbian Dinar (about 2 Euro) for my match ticket. The massive stadium and the heavy police presence were intimidating, but I found my way to the stand behind the goal and sat near to the very vocal supporters of the home side.

I'd been given a tour of the stadium during an advance visit for the World University Games five years earlier, but now, during the game, with supporters roaring for both teams, the entire stadium had come alive. The atmosphere was electric and you couldn't help being swept along with the euphoria of the home supporters. The local favourites Partizan Belgrade won the game and the majority of the supporters went home happy with their team's performance.

I decided to stroll back to the city centre, taking in the sights of downtown Belgrade along the way. The mix of cultures was startling: the combination of old Eastern Bloc style buildings, city centre landmarks still in ruins after the NATO bombing campaign in the old Yugoslavia in the early 90's, and brand new architecture dotted throughout was a little surreal. I arrived back to my now single dorm to find my clothes neatly folded and sitting on my bed. The owner had been busy. It turns out he was a cyclist himself. He understood the perils of a cycle tour and wanted to make my Belgrade experience that little bit more pleasant.

25

DR. ZHIVAGO

Leaving the city the following day, I realised just how hilly the approach to the city is. The energy-sapping rolling hills felt like they would never end. My knee was still quite sore from the crash I'd had a week earlier. After finding a small roadside restaurant in a great location on the bank of the Danube River, I decided to take advantage of what would probably be my last meeting with the lengthy river that had guided me safely through the centre of Europe over the previous weeks.

Getting back on the road after the short break, I realised that the pain in my knee had worsened, all that climbing during the morning had taken its toll, and I wouldn't be going any further that evening, certainly not the 100km I had planned to Jagodina. I booked a bed in the nearby town of Smederevo. I got back on the bike and slowly found my way to the hotel. It was all I could do to collapse on the bed and fall asleep. I couldn't remember being so tired or sore ever in my life.

I decided to take the next day off and organised a massage for the following day. The receptionist at the hotel managed to get me an after-hours appointment with the physiotherapist in the local medical centre. This seemed a much safer bet than my experience earlier in the week in Hungary. That evening, I made the short trip to the medical centre and I asked the physiotherapist to be careful with my knee. At this point, the swelling was pretty intense on the joint. I'd cycled five hundred kilometres in the week since coming off the bike in Hungary and my knee was now screaming at me.

As he made his way around the massage table, his attention kept coming back to my right knee. Eventually, he asked if he could contact the doctor to take a look at it. After a quick phone call in Serbian which sounded particularly ominous, the doctor came through the door and within a minute or so I knew it was more serious than I had expected. He booked me an appointment for the following morning for an ultrasound as he suspected I had fluid on the knee.

I'd been putting off seeking help for the injury in the fear that a doctor might tell me to stop cycling or that my injury was far more serious than I suspected. Yet strangely, it was relief that swept over me now that a doctor was actually taking care of the situation. He instructed the physiotherapist to avoid my legs for the remainder of the session, but the last half hour I almost fell asleep with relief on the massage table.

I was the first patient to see the doctor the following morning. Within minutes, the ultrasound showed that I indeed had some fluid on my knee. It wasn't in an area that posed any long term damage. The scary possibility of having to have the fluid withdrawn with a big syringe had passed and I was instantly more relaxed. He prescribed two days' rest.

I was staying in Smederevo for a few more nights before crossing the border into Bulgaria.

26
SUPER
TROOPERS

The Bulgarian capital, Sofia, was a city I hadn't expected to impress me but as I made my way through the busy streets, the beautiful buildings I was cycling past where extremely impressive.

For the last few days in Serbia and Bulgaria, traffic had been pretty scary. I often found myself on the sometimes non-existent hard shoulder of the main road, or realising I'd gotten closer to flowing traffic than I'd like. I was looking for an alternative route through the rest of Bulgaria. I found an option just north of the main road and decided the following morning I'd try that.

After passing the airport, I took a left turn off the main road and I finally found the nearly-empty roads I wanted. Once again, however, I'd fallen into the trap of not checking elevations, and almost all of the distance that I had to cover went through the mountains to the east of Sofia. Portions of the road had been closed to traffic and fallen into disrepair, with more potholes than I'd ever seen in one place. I even met some local traffic who slalomed their way through the potholes at a crawl.

At the bottom of one descent, I heard dogs barking. To my left, I saw two dogs darting across a farm yard, headed in my direction. I started to increase my speed on the bike and picked up my water bottle in case I needed to squirt water at them. Eventually, I outran the beasts, but not before they'd given me a proper scare.

The remainder of the day saw me climbing and descending the never-ending Bulgarian hills. It wasn't until late afternoon that I realised I hadn't eaten in hours, and then it occurred to me that I hadn't even seen anywhere to get food or drinks all day.

The next major town was seventy kilometres ahead, and I started to worry about the prospects of actually getting food before I'd start to really struggle. There were a number of small villages on the map, but when I passed them by I couldn't see any people, let alone any shops. I was facing a few hours of cycling over hills before I'd actually manage to get to food. Two hours later, I lucked upon a small town with a shop, which I used to stock up on food. I found a spot along the river and sat and watched it flow while I made sure to take in enough sugar to get my tired body over the final hour of the day to Nis.

As I approached the border with Turkey, there was an element of civil unrest being reported from Ankara. Twitter and social media had been banned in the country, and the talk of riots and protests was growing by the day. I did a bit of research and was pretty sure that Istanbul was free of any issues so I kept cycling towards the end of my European odyssey. As I approached the border, I spotted a sign indicating I was merely a few kilometres from the border with Greece. I decided to take a little detour, adding a few kilometres to my day but getting to add another country to my list. Twenty minutes later, I arrived at the Greek border, and with a wave of his hand to my EU passport, the border official has just allowed me across the border.

I've just entered into my fourteenth country of the trip and making my way towards the final country of this leg of the journey, Turkey.

Looking back towards Bulgaria, I noticed the backlog of traffic at the Bulgarian border crossing with Turkey. Just a few hundred metres away, south of the border, I was making great progress east. At least I was until I reached a crest in the road and I spotted a police checkpoint. I was a little surprised when I was pulled over by the police officer. I hadn't seen a sign for no cycling on this road and Google Maps had routed me this direction. After establishing I was an English speaker he spoke to me in fluent English, asking me to remove my backpack and helmet.

"You're not allowed on this road," he said.

"I didn't see any sign saying that, are you sure?" I replied, pretty confident the officer was incorrect.

"There is no cycling allowed on primary roads in Greece," he said, with an extremely serious and slightly intimidating face.

"This isn't a primary road though," I replied. "I thought it was a secondary road."

"It becomes a Motorway further along," he informed me, as one of his colleagues made his way over to see what the hold-up was.

I inspected my map and replied to the officer, saying, "I see that, but that's in one hundred kilometres, I'm leaving the road before that to go to Turkey at Edirne."

I caught the smirk on his partner's face and knew I'd won this battle. With a slightly reluctant and almost disappointed face he handed me back my passport and waved me on, saying, "Make sure you aren't on the road when it becomes a motorway".

Breifne: 1. Greek Police: 0.

*   *   *

I got my helmet back on and as soon as my bag was on my back I took off again. ifteen minutes later the police passed me further along the road. I got a double beep of encouragement from the smirking cop as he drove by. An hour later they had another checkpoint set up. This time, I simply sailed through.

Breifne: 2. Greek Police: 0.

Trying to find Euros to pay for my lunch just shy of the Turkish border was a challenge. On entering Hungary I'd packed my Euro notes and coins away thinking I wouldn't need them for months at the very earliest. Crossing the border was an experience. It was the most intimidating crossing point I'd ever seen, surrounded by heavily armed patrol guards. I had to leave my bike and walk over to a window where the guards quizzed me on my intentions, checked my printed visa, and inspected my passport before they would let me progress.

Cycling away on the Turkish side, I was immediately taken by how many national flags adorned the streets. Nearly every home displayed one, showing the obvious national pride which flowed through this country. Two borders in a single day and my encounters with the Greek police had taken their toll on me, so I found a bed in Edirne and called it a day.

The next few days were spectacular. The hills of western Turkey displayed beautiful farm land as far as the eye could see. After the large distances between towns in parts of Eastern Europe, I was relieved to see regular fuel stops along the highway, which gave me regular options for food and drink. It was at one of these stops that I did a telephone interview with my old sparring partner Martin. We used to co-host a mid-morning radio show on Dublin City FM and now I was one of the invited guests on the show. Martin quizzed me about my journey so far and as I sat in the baking heat in the shade of a petrol station forecourt I realised how far I'd actually come.

The memories of what seemed like a past life flooded through from the other end of the phone line. I realised I wasn't ever going to be able to go back to those days. The journey had already changed me more than I had realised.

27
EASTERN PROMISES

I'd been warned about the approach to Istanbul. A series of inter-linked motorways and highways were perfect for moving the population of Istanbul around at peak times, but as I approached the airport along the coast I found myself in a larger spot of bother than I had anticipated. A four-lane highway was bringing tens of thousands of vehicles into the city during the Friday evening rush hour traffic. Time, or even what day of the week it was, had been immaterial to me for the last month. The only thing that had mattered to me was daylight and border crossing opening times. Everything else had seemed insignificant.

This oversight saw me trying to force myself through the heavy traffic crossing lanes and trying to avoid the highway where possible. I found myself in and out of the main flow of traffic more times than I could keep track. With fast moving traffic on both sides, I eventually found a bike path to the airport and managed to avoid the bulk of the traffic.

I finally made it to Ataturk International Airport as dusk was setting in. The cycling element of the first stage of the journey was now complete. I just had to work out how to get myself and my bike to India now.

I made my way through the small tight streets of the Turkish capital and reached the hostel I had booked online. With the political and military unrest in the Middle East, the rules of the race allowed me to fly over countries that posed a security risk. That meant flying from Turkey to India, skipping over Syria, Iraq, Iran, Pakistan and Afghanistan.

I needed to sort out a bike box for my flight the next day. I ate and got an early night before spending a day of playing the tourist around the city. I'd been refusing to cut my hair or shave since starting the race because I'd been planning a Turkish shave once I'd reached Istanbul and completed the first continent on my list.

I found a barber who offered a Turkish shave. As it turns out, it's not as common as you'd think. Now that I looked reasonably respectable, I set off to find a bike box. It turns out you can't just rock up at the airport and load your bike on the plane as baggage, you have a bit of preparation and packing to do first. I'd found a flight I wanted to book, it was under budget but was later on that evening. I held off on booking the flight until I was certain I'd be able to make it. It took five bike shops before I found a suitable box. When I say box, I mean literally that. All I was looking for was the kind of cardboard box that a new bike comes in from the manufacturer, and most shops dispose of their boxes immediately.

When I finally managed to get my box back through the centre of town, I couldn't get the pedals off the bike. This would prove to be my downfall a number of times on the trip. With the handlebars and saddle removed, the attached pedals are almost twice as wide as the rest of the bike. Because they are designed to tighten as you pedal the bike, they become very difficult to remove without specialised equipment. My small pedal wrench just wasn't going to cut it. I grabbed a lift with one of the hostel staff, with my bike and my box, back to the bike shop. The guy smirked at me as I came back to him obviously suspecting I might return. Twenty minutes later at the cost of ten Euros, my bike was securely packed up in its new home and ready to fly to India.

I booked the flight and my bus to the airport for the following day once I got back to the hostel. As I sat at the computer in the communal area I got talking to one of the local guys, who took a huge interest in my story.

After a few hours chatting in the hostel we made our way into the town to look around and maybe catch a drink, we ended up in a karaoke bar where we both joined the locals in singing a few tunes and having a few drinks.

We ended up meeting a group of men in the bar who after an hour or so suggested we move somewhere else. My hostel buddy was working the following day and he made his way home, but I decided to stay with the guys I'd just met. We had too many for a single taxi so I got in the first one with one of the men leaving the other three standing on the kerb heading to the new location.

The taxi pulled up outside a hotel and my new friend guided me up a flight of stairs into a dark room quarter full of people dotted around at tables, I sat at the table I was directed to by the attractive hostess who had greeted us at the door. Within a few seconds she had beckoned two of her colleagues to join us. She sat down beside me and started to speak to me in perfect English. Her male colleague took our order, and within ninety seconds of sitting down we were surrounded by drinks and a table full of food. I was deeply confused by the sudden appearance of three stunning women who had attached themselves to our little group.

Now I know I'm devilishly handsome, but I'm certainly not used to this level of attention from the kinds of girls I tend to see on the front page of glossy magazines. I asked my 'friend' when his other friends would arrive and he didn't really answer my question and finally the penny dropped. I'd been duped into one of those situations you hear about back home.

I explained to the hostess that there had been a mistake, and that I was looking to leave, she left to get the manager, bringing the other girls for moral support. When the manager came over he had a bill for over €650 with him. I would have laughed nervously if three guys much bigger than anyone I'd ever seen before hadn't just entered the room through various doors. My mind was racing at this point. The manager blocked my route to the main door, but one of the heavies was stationed there anyway.

"I simply ordered a coke," I said to the manager.

He responded in perfect English, saying, "This is the bill for the group, you, your friend, the girls, and the food."

"I didn't order the food," I replied. "I don't actually know this guy, he's certainly not a friend. I'm not paying for any of that other than the Coke that I ordered."

The guy looked at me, looked at the boss and got up and walked away. The manager's lack of reaction confirmed to me that the whole situation was a set-up.

He pointed at a sign nicely hidden to the side of the door informing me that it was compulsory to purchase a drink for a girl as well as myself. I gulped.

"Okay, I've fallen into your trap," I said. "You're going to get some money out of me, I don't want my arms or legs broken and, let's be honest, you don't want to deal with the police tomorrow. I'll pay for my drink and the cheapest drink that the girls ordered."

He looked at me, shocked. "I have a club to run, you can't just walk out without paying," he said.

I reminded him of my offer to pay for my drink and one other. I worked it out to €60, going by the exorbitant menu that was still on the table. €10 for the coke and €50 for the cheapest alcoholic drink on the menu, less than one tenth of the amount he was seeking.

We eventually settled on a price of around €150, I'm pretty sure that me being stone cold sober was the reason he was so eager to get me out of the club. Had I been under the influence I'd have been easier to convince to share the wealth.

I only had about 20 Euros worth of Turkish Lira on me so I offered one of my debit cards, knowing full well there was only just about that amount of money available on the card. He refused as they didn't have a card machine. I wasn't surprised by this at all, and thought I might have found my get out of jail free card. He insisted on taking a taxi with me to a nearby ATM machine, the fear was now rising in my stomach. What had I gotten myself into? I explained I'd go along with it on the basis that no one would follow or accompany me to the machine. He agreed and we set off.

He sat in the passenger seat and I was in the back on my own as he spoke to the driver. We pulled up across the road from a bank and I went to the machine, took out the cash and once back in the cab gave the agreed amount to the club manager.

We made our way back towards the club in the cab and the entire time he was trying to convince me that I could spend the night with his hostess for the bargain-basement price of €1,000. I actually laughed now, much more secure that he wasn't going to hurt me.

I politely refused and after he got out of the cab at the club, he insisted that the taxi bring me back to my hotel. Worried that I might not be safe I gave him a fake address and he dropped me off at the door of a random hotel in the main tourist district about half a mile from where I was actually staying. I left the cab and entered the hotel, waiting for him to disappear around the next corner before setting off for my actual room.

I double locked the door that night and barely slept. I was pretty happy to be getting out of town the next day, I was leaving the madness and insecurity of Istanbul and heading to India, I sincerely hoped I wasn't jumping from the frying pan into the fire.

INDIA

7th April - 12th June, 2014

MUMBAI

GOA

BANGALORE

CHENNAI

KOLKATA

VISAKHAPATNAM

Distance: 3,557km

Elevation: 18,687 metres

28

A PASSAGE
TO INDIA

"4:27 AM" flashed back at me from the screen of my phone. How was it so warm in the pitch black of an Indian night? I could see the city of Mumbai, bright in the distance as I walked out of the airport terminal. Prasad, the sole Indian entrant in the World Cycle Race, was beaming a massive smile back at me from the other side of the greeting area. He had brought a few friends with him in order to welcome me to his country.

Prasad's visa issues had continued, and without access to Europe it was not possible for him to continue in the race. In addition to Fran withdrawing in the first week, the World Cycle Race was down to three riders, which meant that I was guaranteed a podium place in the race just by finishing.

We talked as I rebuilt the bike in a car park opposite the terminal. Traffic was pretty chaotic leaving the airport so I elected to walk along with Prasad for about ten minutes to get to a quieter spot while my GPS device tried to recognise my location.

It was a little after day break now. The vista was brightening up around me as the sun rose in the sky. Women dressed in traditional saree were carrying bricks on a nearby building site as the men threw dirty looks back at me. Prasad warned me not to look at the women as it could be seen as disrespectful to their husbands. I was a little thrown by this but decided to err on the side of caution and turned my attention to my bike changed my clothes, and faced into the distance, across the bustling city.

Once I finally got the bike assembled and abdicated all directional decisions to Prasad, I was much more comfortable. The heat was still phenomenal, much hotter than anything I'd ever experienced before. Prasad had kindly offered to act in a support capacity for a few days until we reached his home town of Wai at the very least. His van would become a very familiar sight in the distance in the chaotic streets of Mumbai. His tactic of staying about ten to twenty car lengths ahead of me meant I felt like I was always playing catch up. It was difficult to stay in touch at times, as the thronged streets didn't appear to have any rules. Decrepit cars, rickshaws, motorbikes, overcrowded buses, animals and humans were headed in all directions. Little attention was paid by anyone to the rules of the road in any way, shape or form.

Have I mentioned the smell?

The smell was overpowering, and not in a good way. Some streets appeared filthier than others, but they shared the odour regardless of how they looked. It was a mixture of decaying food, dead animals, excrement and urine which wafted through the air and burned the inside of my nostrils. Luckily for me it meant the super sweaty, lycra-clad cyclist blended right in most of the time, even in massive crowds.

The endless turns down overcrowded streets continued for most of the morning, until we hit one of the main highways around the city. Having a personal GPS device in the shape of a small van a few hundred metres ahead of me was certainly beginning to make my job a lot easier. Decisions had been removed from my world. All I had to do was follow the leader.

As we reached the other side of the sprawling city of Mumbai and set off on the old highway towards the city of Pune and Prasad's home town, I was really beginning to feel both the hunger and jet lag attack at the same time.

Prasad pulled off the road and we found a spot under the shade of a tree where we all slept for an hour, I woke covered in sweat but feeling much better, albeit still hungry.

We found a McDonalds, a reasonably rare occurrence in India, especially outside the major cities. This stop gave me the chance to get my bearings from Google Maps while stocking up on whatever it was they called a sausage. It certainly didn't resemble anything I'd ever seen described as a sausage before.

I'm not very adventurous when it comes to meal time. My tastes are very Irish. Meat and two vegetables or steak and chips would be my go-to options on a menu. I don't really like to experiment with food so I suspected India, Thailand and Malaysia were going to be challenging due to not having rice on my approved list.

Here I was, in the safe option of a western fast food outlet, the fear of what I was going to eat for the next six weeks across the country was just beginning to grow from concern to panic.

Even though I was in a country where I couldn't speak the language, I didn't look like anyone else around me and I was slightly scared of the food options. Some things prove how small the world can be.

As I ordered my sausage, the kid serving me asked me where I was from. I pointed at my green, white and gold jersey and said "Ireland". His next question was about cricket. I mentioned that I knew a few guys and girls who played cricket for Ireland. His eyes lit up as the name "Kevin O'Brien" left his mouth, I smiled back.

Kevin was one of the most exciting players in Irish cricket in recent years, setting a World Cup record for the quickest century in Ireland's defeat of England in 2011. It seemed as if Kevin was a bit of a household name in India despite being virtually unknown in Ireland. Kevin and I had crossed paths a number of times in recent years. I had been coaching a football team in Railway Union for the previous two years, and during the overlap between football and cricket season, Kevin was coaching another group of kids in the same grounds and we shared the training space. I had interviewed him a number of times for both TV and radio shows I'd been presenting, and it turns out we also shared a birthday.

I told the kid behind the counter that I knew Kevin and I might as well have said that I was best friends with David Beckham, Messi or Cristiano Ronaldo. My street cred had just blown through the roof. A barrage of questions about Irish cricket followed, most of which I was unable to answer before I tucked into my meal.

After starting the climb into the Western Ghats, the jet lag came back in force. We had hoped to reach Pune that night, but it must have slipped Prasad's mind to mention the small matter of the high mountain range, the Western Ghats, between Mumbai and the other main city in the state of Maharashtra. On reaching the hilltop town of Lonavala, I knew my legs weren't capable of going any further that day. There was a lovely hotel on the far side of the road, but Prasad was eager to find us something more affordable. After a few efforts of finding a 'lodge' for the night I convinced him that the fifteen Euros for the nights' accommodation was fine. On my first night in India, I just wanted a good night's sleep.

* * *

The next two days consisted of climbing until we reached Prasad's home town of Wai. I had been invited to stay with Prasad's family in their home, and their hospitality was pretty special. When I was greeted at the door by Prasad's mother, she performed a welcome ritual which involved candles and dabbing a mixture on my forehead with her thumb. After issuing the greeting, his father also welcomed me to his home. On entering the bathroom, I went looking for the shower, but I couldn't find it. It was then that I spotted the bucket and jug in the corner of the bathroom.

I filled the large bucket with cold water and used the jug to pour it over my body. The cold water was particularly refreshing after a long day in the saddle in the searing Indian sun. Even the cockroach who decided to join me briefly in the shower couldn't dampen my mood in such a friendly and inviting atmosphere. I slept very well in Prasad's room that evening.

Leaving the van at home, Prasad had offered to cycle with me for another day. His wife worked in a city over one hundred kilometres away, back on the coast side of the mountain range. It meant another day climbing back over the hills I'd crossed the previous two days, but although I wasn't excited about the prospect of returning to climbing I'd promised my cousin Aidan I was going to visit Goa, which was on the ocean and south of Wai. Prasad's wife and daughter lived along the way, and I was looking forward to having the company.

We seemed to be climbing for the entire day until we crested the mountain range. The view on the far side of the mountain was simply out of this world. The road moved swiftly beneath me as I passed through areas of jungle with monkeys swinging, to open views of the valley stretching as far as the eye could see. The sheer drops into the valley off to the left hand side of the road were concerning at times. There was only a simple foot-high barrier to keep me from certain injury if I got too close to the edge. After a breath-taking forty minutes descending the mountain we made our way through the flatlands towards the town of Chiplun, where I finally said good bye to Prasad.

29
HIT THE ROAD JACK

Over the next few days, I made my way south along the Indian coast with Goa in mind. The rolling hills slowed me down somewhat, but all the detours and climbs were worth it to keep the beautiful ocean in my sight for most of the evening. I decided to stay off the main roads where possible to avoid the crazy traffic, and had long stretches in the wilderness where no people or buildings were there to disturb the peace and quiet of the Indian countryside. It seemed worlds away from the hustle and bustle of Mumbai or Pune. In a country with over one billion people, it was amazing that huge areas of the coastal regions were devoid of any development.

Late one evening, I found myself approaching the coastal town of Ratnagiri. It still amazes me how regions and cities in India with larger populations than Northern Ireland or other small European countries aren't even on our radar on my side of the world.

As I approached the town, traffic started to slow until it came to an absolute stop. It seemed I'd arrived bang smack in the middle of the local festival or fair. Budget accommodation was already completely snapped up and I was directed towards the sea front, which boasted a number of properties that were more likely to have vacancies. The hotel at the pier looked as if it was still under construction, but once inside the luxury was pretty evident. I managed to negotiate the price down to about 1,500 rupees or just under 20 Euros for the night's stay in an ocean facing, air conditioned room with a fabulous balcony where I sat sipping a cold drink while the sun set over the ocean.

Next door was a small restaurant where I recognised an American guy I'd spotted at the hotel reception earlier. He was also travelling alone, although his trip was for work. I asked him if I could join him to eat. I chatted with Andy for hours over a few drinks, as we sampled the local cuisine. I was getting better at selecting meals from the menu, although the super spicy selections were always a no-go for me. My palette had at least stretched to a chicken tandoori and some naan bread or some other chicken option without the spicy sauces.

I left Andy's company and went to bed, I was super excited about the following two days. I'd found a tree house on Anjuna Beach in north Goa that I had booked for two nights for just two hundred rupees – a little over two Euro. I just had the small task of crossing the two hundred kilometres between me and the idyllic setting which awaited me.

I woke bright and early, oblivious to the fact that this was going to be the hardest day of my journey so far. The heat the day before had sapped all my energy. I'd only managed to cover little over eighty kilometres, and now faced a lot of work to make it to my tree house on Anjuna Beach.

I was on the bike at dawn, and rolling just before seven. The temperatures in the middle of the day had become unbearably hot, and as the hours passed the heat grew until it was once again virtually impossible to keep my body heat at a level with which I could cope. The locals obviously had the same idea, and with nobody visible on the streets I had the countryside to myself. Short breaks were necessary every hour or so to cool down. I was unable to keep enough water stocks on the bike I was stopping at every opportunity to refill bottles and top up my own water levels. In this heat, I was consuming about two litres of water for every hour in the saddle.

On reaching the seaside village of Malvan, I found a small lodge where the guy let me snooze through the midday heat in one of the rooms. Laying on a bed in an air conditioned room with the view of the deserted beach just a stone's throw away and the waves of the blue ocean beyond it lapping at the sand was phenomenal. I managed about two or three hours sleep before getting back on the road.

Within a few minutes of restarting in the afternoon, a guy on a motorbike pulled up alongside me. He started firing questions at me like so many others, but on hearing my origin point he became particularly interested. He told me he was a reporter for the local paper and would like to interview me for his newspaper and offered to buy me a cup of tea. I accepted and joined him, and half an hour later I was finally rolling again. I had nearly a hundred kilometres to get to Anjuna and with only two hours of daylight remaining, I knew I was going to be in the dark for a long period this evening.

A few hours after dark I was still on the road, but I'd made the decision to continue until I reached my tree house. I'd planned a few days off in Goa and didn't want to lose a day's rest because I couldn't make today's distance. I finally reached the Terekhol River, the border between Goa and Maharashtra, at 10 pm, where

I was stopped by the border guards and quizzed briefly about my intentions before it became clear they weren't interested in me as I wasn't smuggling any contraband items into the state. I was simply waved through the checkpoint with the message that Anjuna was only a few kilometres away ringing in my ears.

The information the guards told me didn't tally with what I had expected. I was facing into a further thirty kilometres which, at today's pace, would mean at least another two hours before I get to bed. It was almost three hours before I reached Anjuna. It turned out the name Anjuna applied to a fairly wide area, so it took some persuading to get specific directions.

At one in the morning I reached the coast and starting asking people for directions to the tree houses. Two guys who were just dismantling their burger shop gave me great directions and I even spotted a sign for the place I was looking for. Despite this I managed to get lost again in the dark.

That's when I spotted the girl standing outside a house just ahead on the side of the road. I should have guessed from the state of her swollen eye balls and her jaw grating on itself, but I'm pretty sure she was under the influence of something stronger than alcohol. She started roaring obscenities and personal insults at me, suggesting I was threatening her and asking why I was asking for directions in the dark, implying there was something sinister going on.

I cut my losses and started to cycle away when something hit me on my back, she'd just started throwing stones at me, another one whizzed past my helmet before I managed to get out of her throwing range, although I could still hear her verbal abuse carrying on the ocean breeze. Just under a kilometre further along the road I almost cycled into a sign for my tree house. The actual bedroom, or platform to be completely accurate, was as amazing as I'd imagined. Mind you, any resting place would have been great after eighteen hours on the road. I could hear the ocean just metres away from me beyond the open curtain which circled the bamboo platform I was sleeping on, two stories above the ground.

The following day I woke with the sunshine beaming into my face. Turning my head towards the right I could just see the palm trees which held countless platforms and bamboo ladders joining it all together. Beyond the dark green foliage I could spot the blue of the ocean, the golden sand and the foaming white waves where the two met. I had heard the waves the previous night but actually taking in the vista was something else.

I slowly came to and made my way down to the restaurant for breakfast, situated just under the palm trees along the edge of the beach it was the perfect location to relax. I picked up a copy of the classic novel *To Kill a Mockingbird* from the library of books and started re-reading Harper Lee for the first time since I'd studied her for my Junior Cert in school.

It was at that moment that it hit me. I was sitting on a bean bag, sipping on a fruit juice, book in hand with a view of the Indian Ocean. Life really doesn't get much better than this.

30
EVERYBODY'S FREE TO WEAR SUNSCREEN

Twenty four hours was long enough to spend in Anjuna. One of the British tourists I'd met over lunch had suggested Palolem Beach to the south. It was on my route, so I figured I'd split my days off between the two locations. I got back in the saddle and made the short 85 kilometre trip from the northern end of the state of Goa to the south. This was obviously a more popular destination, and it was harder to find a place to stay, but I found a room just away from the beach at the Castle Hotel.

With the restaurant and the pool just beside my room, I was tempted not to leave for the next twenty four hours, but I changed my mind after falling into a conversation with two other residents, an English guy named Joe who was a teacher in Thailand and an Italian girl turned American college professor Chiara. The three of us had been put at separate adjoining tables for breakfast but had sparked up conversations with each other. Chiara left to meet friends that had come on the overnight bus from Bangalore, so Joe and I hung out for the evening and we decided to hit the beach.

We weren't sitting longer than ten minutes when Chiara wandered over with her three friends, Grace, Danielle and Malin. The girls were college students on foreign exchange for a semester from Vermont, Arizona and Sweden, respectively and Chiara was one of their professors in Christ University in Bangalore. We chatted for the entire evening before we called it a night.

Danielle talked about how she was petrified of the open ocean so she eventually was dared to face her fear. I admitted I also wasn't great in deep water and it was decided that the entire group was going to try their hand at sea kayaking the following day. Joe had to catch his flight home so I made my way down to the girls and before I even had time to think about it I found myself sitting on a kayak headed towards the oncoming breaking waves. I fell in at the first attempt of breaking through. Not a great start. The nerves were building into a real fear now. Grace and Danielle were already half way out to sea in their kayak while Chiara and Malin had just left me on my own on the shore line. I was having second thoughts about whether I really wanted to continue but I wasn't going to let a few waves get in my way.

I sat back on the top of the kayak and set off straight for the incoming swell. This time around I hit the wave perfectly straight, paddling frantically, and when I opened my eyes there was nothing but clear ocean ahead of me. Much to my own surprise, I was still on top of the kayak. I continued to paddle until I was certain I'd passed the point where the waves might break. Looking around at the crescent beach behind me and the open Indian Ocean laid out in front of me, I saw that the girls had already set off towards the small island to the right hand side of the bay made famous by Matt Damon's early morning run in *The Bourne Supremacy*. I followed suit and quickly caught up with both boats. I was still a little uncertain about my balance and half expected to find myself in the water before too long.

We spent an hour and a half roaming around the bay - far enough off shore that we couldn't really distinguish the bars and restaurants from each other and the tourists on the sand appeared like little ants. One or two of the girls jumped in for a dip to cool off.

I'd stupidly decided not to wear a t-shirt, which seemed like a good idea in the mid-morning when we left shore. In the glaring midday heat, I could feel my skin getting hotter and hotter. Of course I managed to capsize the boat and face planted into the water in the shallow surf as we got back to the beach, but nevertheless, I was thrilled to have taken on one of my biggest fears and survived. Danielle, too, was beaming with pride after her little adventure.

Within a few hours I had truly come to regret not wearing a t-shirt. I was struggling to move my arms and shoulders without wincing in pain as my upper body turned a beautiful shade of tomato red. After a freezing cold shower, I was lying face down on my bed under the ceiling fan, which was rotating so fast I thought it might take off, and I was as hot as I'd been out in the mid-day sun. I knew cycling the next day wasn't going to be an option. There was no way I was going to be able to wear my backpack on my shoulders in this condition.

To be fair, the girls looked after me, applying after sun to the areas of my back I couldn't reach and walking super slow as we found a place to eat that evening. Chiara then invited me to come speak to the remainder of her class in Bangalore about my journey. I agreed to the slight route change before I actually checked the terrain involved. It would mean a third, but final, pass over the Western Ghats.

31
EVERYDAY IS A
WINDING ROAD

After three relaxing and fun days in Palolem, I finally decided to hit the road the fourth day. As I was packing my bag I got a tweet from Dylan, an English cycle fanatic who'd been in London at the start line of the race. As luck would have it, he'd just arrived in Goa for his holiday. He asked if I was free for a drink so I invited him for an early lunch before I set off. Our longer-than-planned lunch took about four hours, during which I sat with Dylan and his friend Georg chatting and swapping stories. They had both visited India a number of times including a road trip up the east coast from Chennai to Kolkata, which was the journey I was facing into in just a few weeks. I tried to soak up all the information.

Before too long I had settled my bill, a 'pricey' sixty five Euro for three nights' accommodation, including three meals each day. More importantly, I was back on the road. The two boys followed me in the car for a few kilometres before I finally said goodbye and turned south towards Mangalore, while they headed back towards their own hotel. I dreaded the next ten or fifteen kilometres of climbing into the hills, which every local I'd spoken to had mentioned over the previous few days.

Usually, my body won't wake up until I've had eight hours of sleep. It's both a blessing and a curse. I'm usually well-rested when I wake up, but unfortunately it means I have a habit of sleeping through alarms, doorbells, college exams and doctor's appointments. The best thing about crossing Europe in this regard was the check-out time at my various lodgings. In a situation where I had slept through my alarm, the staff of the hostel would pester me until I eventually heard them and get myself out of dodge. Most of the places I stayed in India had no such thing as a check out time. No matter what time I arrived at my lodgings, the room was mine until the same time the following day. My body clock had a field day with this custom, but it played havoc with my progress, costing me half days in places or sometimes even complete days.

Leaving the coastal highway in Mangalore, I had my target set on Bangalore. I'd agreed to do the talk there in just a few days but I had the small matter of navigating the Western Ghats again. This would be the first solo attempt. I spent two days working my way slowly into the foothills before the heavy day-long climbing was due to start. I found a cheap hotel just past the village of Nellyadi. A river flowing behind the hotel offered some peace although it was tempered by the constant noise from the highway at the front of the hotel.

I fell asleep and set my alarm clock for 5am. I knew I needed to be on the road early the following day, it would be the toughest climb so far and with no evidence of any towns or villages on the road I was going to have to stock up on supplies and water. It was still dark when the alarm woke me up. After getting my bearings, I made my way to the main road and started cycling. I'd gone nearly twenty kilometres before dawn broke over the mountains ahead of me. I found a small breakfast at the final service station at Shiradi and stocked up on food, eager to get cracking on the climb that was just about to turn serious. I was delighted with my decision to launch into the early morning before the sun really got warmed up. Every hour or so on the climb I was stopping to eat and drink a little, and each time it was one hour closer to midday and a little hotter than the previous stop. With no shade or cloud cover in sight and with the mid-day heat fast approaching, I reached for the water bottle to find it bone dry, I'd drank it all.

My food levels were dangerously low, too. Eventually I found a bit of shade under a parked truck, I could hear a mountain stream flowing in the small valley just below the road and after much consideration about the potential toxins and the very real chances of contracting a bout of Delhi Belly, I decided it was more important to get fluids in. I could deal with the sickness if it came, as I'd planned for it and had medication with me to deal with diarrhoea or vomiting if either should arise.

I took my water bottles and climbed down off the road to the stream. I consumed the first bottle in record time, and I could feel my body temperature reducing by the time I'd got the second bottle into me. I sipped the third before climbing back up the short but steep incline to my bicycle and my bags with full water bottles.

32
THE GOOD SAMARITAN

The short break and the fluids helped me keep going, but less than an hour later I ran out again. This time, it was more troubling. My energy levels were low. I had been struggling to stay upright on the bike and had been reduced to pushing the bike up the hill ahead of me at a snail's pace.

The only thought going through my mind was of the hill, how it snaked up ahead of me. I couldn't get one thought out of my head though. I knew that it was all plain sailing downhill behind me, to the place I had breakfast 30 kilometres beforehand. I wouldn't even have to pedal the entire way. I could freewheel down and be there in less than half an hour.

I'd covered almost fifty kilometres that morning already, although most of the last four hours had been slower than walking pace up the side of the mountain. Here I found myself, eight weeks into my journey, way behind schedule and struggling to cope with the terrain, the weather and the distances.

* * *

For the first time since Greenwich, I was thinking about quitting. I stood and stared at the road rising ahead of me. I had absolutely no idea how long this went on for. I was only half way up in terms of my projected altitude gain, but that could be a handful of kilometres steeply or a constant rise for the next fifty kilometres.

I was just about to give in to my urge to turn around and call the entire thing off and head home. Unlike the Levite in Jesus' parable of the Good Samaritan, I might not have been stripped and beaten, but I probably did look half dead as I struggled to walk up the hill.

It was just at that moment that my very own Good Samaritan pulled in ahead of me. An Indian man stepped out of his car and walked the short distance back to where I had stopped.

"You look like you need help," he said.

I summoned the energy to nod my head and said, "Yes, I've run out of water and food."

"I can bring you to the next town if you wish?" he offered.

"Sorry, but I can't accept as I'm in a race and would be disqualified," I replied.

The man walked to the rear of his car and started looking through the contents of his car boot as I heard him explain to his wife what was going on. I could see a bag in one hand and a bottle of water in the other as he turned to come back down the hill to me. I wasn't even able to close the gap between where I was standing and the car, it was a mere thirty metres, but it felt like a few kilometres in my condition. The litre of water was gone down my neck in seconds.

Arvind, as he had introduced himself, then handed me the bag from his other hand and I took a look through the contents, cookies, biscuits, crackers and other snacks as he went back to the car for more water. I filled up my water bottle and then emptied it again.

Arvind was a cyclist himself, living in Bangalore, and had spotted the signs of my struggle as he passed me along the road. He gave me his phone number and wrote down a list of places I could get my bike serviced in Bangalore. Before he left me, we agreed to meet up when I reached the city.

I got back in the saddle. Although I still wasn't sure about how far the journey was ahead of me I managed to make slow but steady progress upwards. As I turned the next series of bends I spotted an old stone building on the side of the road.

Although it looked like a ruin, the tell-tale signs of a small constant flow of water running towards me from a hand wash area on the far side of the entrance, the sign for a local beer displayed on the road side and the packets of potato crisps hanging outside were promising. I nearly sprinted up the hill towards the shack, and the shade and sustenance it might provide.

The place was deserted with no signs of life. I decided to help myself to the crisps and picked a bottle of coke from the bucket behind the counter leaving more than enough cash on the counter. I sat in the shade and tried to understand how close I'd come to quitting and the turn of events that had kept me going.

After climbing a mountain range for hours and hours in the searing heat, I had been about to pull the plug just a few metres shy of my destination. This roadside shack was obviously not my final destination, but it had become a vital checkpoint on my way. It allowed me to gather my thoughts, refuel, rehydrate, and plan my assault on the rest of my journey.

My thoughts were interrupted by the landlord joining me. He'd been off tending to his animals on the small farm behind the restaurant. He didn't speak a word of English, but I managed to order from his menu and within ten minutes I was filling my face with a freshly cooked chicken dinner. It tasted ten times better than anything I'd ever eaten in my life.

Between eating, curling up for a sleep on a wooden bench in the bar and trying to avoid the direct midday sun, I stayed there for about three hours all told. My pattern of riding in the early morning, a long lazy lunch, and getting back on the bike in the evening was proving a much better recipe for getting plenty of mileage into the legs each day.

After two lunches and copious amounts of water and soft drinks, I set off again once the main heat had been taken out of the day. I had hoped to hit Aluru or Hassan this evening but that goal wasn't realistic anymore.

I decided to change my plans and set my target on Sakleshpur, just twenty kilometres ahead. Although I was still climbing, there was a little respite with some downhill sections before I rolled into town. A local wedding would mean accommodation was at a premium, but eventually I found a place just a short walk from the town centre.

The food in the restaurant next door was vegetarian so I went off in the hopes of finding a non-vegetarian option. I found a place and tucked into a good serving of chicken. The range of meats eaten in India isn't amazing. Pork is seldom on the menu and beef is non-existent due to the sacred status bestowed on cows all over the sub-continent.

The pace of life in every town is dictated by the cows who wander freely around the street, amongst the traffic where motorists must wait for the cow to move on before they progress. It's chaos to someone from the western world, but it works well for the Indian people.

As I left the restaurant, I remembered that I needed to pick up some toiletries. In the dark, I walked across the road to the street side pharmacy, and as I was waiting in the line it started to rain and suddenly people started to run in all directions.

Within thirty seconds I knew exactly why. The light rain had turned into a downpour. Sheets of rain were visibly falling from the sky and the water was bouncing back off the ground. Some of the locals just walked along as if it was a summer's day while the majority sought shelter under awnings and in doorways.

The street-side traders pulled their tables back into their premises to create more dry space as people just continued to flood in from all angles.

Within a few minutes the thunder and lightning had joined the party and we were facing into a full monsoon style storm. The dark night sky had gotten even blacker and the normally cloudless night sky looked angry and ominous above the town.

Fifteen minutes later the last of the rain fell. People dissipated back into the dark where they had come from. I was left on my own under the awning of the pharmacy, looking at the newly formed rivers streaming down both sides of the street in front of me.

Concerned that another storm might interrupt my short walk back to the room, I ran most of the way along the now-deserted streets. Less than an hour after it started, it was as if the rain had never happened. People, motorbikes, cars and rickshaws were clogging up the street. There was no sign of moisture on the roads or in the fields around the hotel and the noise of people, animals and traffic was once again everywhere.

33
GUESS WHO'S COMING TO DINNER

A few days later I was standing in front of Chiara's class in Christ University in Bangalore. It was a very informal discussion about my journey, where I showed a few videos of my trip so far and explained the reasons behind it. What was meant to be a fifteen minute presentation was still active with questions and answers two hours later, an hour after the class was due to be finished.

I ended up heading for lunch with Chiara and a few of the students and we made plans to meet up again that evening to sample some of the night life that Bangalore had to offer.

Chiara was a fantastic host for my few days in the city. She had booked a few days in Sri Lanka which meant that other than the first day she was actually out of the country and I had the full run of her place just around the corner from the school.

I took the opportunity to take a rest, my body still recovering from the day climbing the Western Ghats earlier in the week. The one thing she had warned me about was the rickshaw drivers. Seeing white skin, they usually refuse to use their metres to calculate the fare. They appear to have an agreement between themselves of overcharging. It might take asking twenty drivers to find one who would agree to do it for the right price.

Now in the grand scheme of things you're talking about the difference between €1 and €3 for a fare that would cost you €15 - €30 in a taxi at home, but it's the principle of these drivers looking at western faces as a cash machine that matters.

You could practically see the dollar signs ringing up like a slot machine when they saw you approaching them.

Chiara would get very agitated with the drivers and would take the half hour to ask a vast number of drivers before agreeing with one who would do it. While I think she was right, I wasn't prepared to spend twenty minutes and bundles of energy on arguing with random Indians. My tactic was to get into the first rickshaw and offer to pay whatever the metre displayed plus a fifty percent tip. After a bit of haggling, a threat to report them to the authorities normally sealed the deal.

I was pleasantly surprised by the evening in Bangalore. I was invited to a birthday party for two of the girls in the class and I joined them in a very fancy restaurant just two doors down from Chiara's place. I spent most of the evening chatting to the three girls I'd met in Goa and Parker, a Californian in the girl's class who had been one of the more active participants in the questions and answers section of my presentation.

I had taken the time to research the terrain towards Chennai. Common sense would suggest that going from a point almost a kilometre above sea level to the coast would involve a huge help from gravity. I wasn't to be disappointed, but even better than facing into the drop in a few quick sharp bursts I was facing a very small downward gradient for the entire distance. I suspected that I could break my own personal record for a single day.

In the first few weeks across Europe I'd come very close to exceeding 200km for the day, but that had been done with the assistance of having a support car carrying the majority of my luggage.

Here, I was looking into three hundred downward kilometres and I knew that with an early start I could finally get across that 200km stumbling block. I had planned my route out of the city and back onto the main road towards Hosur, Krishnagiri & Vellore. The streets were practically empty at half past six when I set off heading away from the Dairy Circle, a major roundabout which had been my landmark when returning to Chiara's apartment.

I found myself following the route I had planned when road signs directed me onto an elevated road. I was already on the raised causeway when I realised it wasn't designed for bikes. Luckily it was still the early hours of the morning, and I had avoided the major rush hour.

At the end of the six kilometre road there was a toll plaza. I kept left and expected to pass through without payment as I had done so often on the national roads up to this point. The toll operator looked at me as if to say "Where did you come from? You're not supposed to be on this road."

I tried explaining that I hadn't intended it but that my passage had been accidental. He made up a figure of 30 rupees (40 cent) and insisted I pay before he would permit me to pass through the barrier. That price wasn't on display on the signage and I suspect it was just a bit of opportunistic personal money grabbing by the toll operator.

I didn't really mind, the money was tiny and I'd avoided the entire nightmare of the ridiculously busy city streets of Bangalore. I was headed east and making great time.

The rest of the day is a little bit of a blur, I spent most of the next fourteen hours in the saddle, aside from my now-habitual siesta to get out of the mid-day heat.

I was keeping an eye on the figures clocking up over the course of the day on the Garmin device in front of me. I clocked up the first hundred kilometres in well under four hours.

I'd made 206.6km by the time I pulled into my hotel on the side of the road. After checking in to my room and showering, I was invited by the group of Indian men sitting outside the hotel to join them for dinner. The experience was great. Watching them mix and match meats, rice and sauces across a range of meals was delightful. The supply of food seemed endless.

Despite the lack of English, I quickly established that the man who had invited me to join the group was the owner of the hotel and that the remainder of the men were the elders of the community. The local doctor, judge and chief of police were included in the half dozen men.

At the end of the banquet, I wasn't permitted to pay for any of the food. The owner just waved his hand at me and turned away issuing orders to the staff scurrying around at his beck and call.

The next day I had the relatively simple task of finishing the downhill stretch to the coast at Chennai. I was beginning to suspect that my body might throw a spanner in the works.

I'd begun to feel a little bit sick in the previous forty eight hours and I was worried I was coming down with Delhi Belly. I wasn't quite sure how cycling cross country would fit with the need to be within a few metres of a toilet all day long.

The inevitable finally happened as I got within spitting distance of Chennai. I could feel the pressure building as I reached Bagavelli and eventually after much sign language translation I found a place to stay. I made my way through a small tunnel between two buildings to find two older Indian guys sitting around a fire. I negotiated a price I was happy with and asked to see the room before committing to the deal. Both men decided to show me upstairs to the room, which was awful. I'd stayed in some pretty bad places so far across India but this was by far and away the worst I'd seen. I knew I didn't have a whole lot of time to make a decision, as the building pressure in my gut was beginning to get a bit more intense.

I indicated to the guy who looked like the boss, against my better judgement, that I'd take the room for the agreed price, and reached for the money from my wallet. As I was doing this the other guy got involved, started talking animatedly, and found his English in the shape of a price that was double what we had agreed beforehand.

This started a row between the two Indian men, one happy to take the agreed price for the room, the other trying to milk every last rupee out of the white man now sitting on the bed in the middle of the room. I got an uneasy feeling about the entire place. Firstly the dirt had been off-putting but now I suspected the two guys had been sampling some substances sitting around the fire below.

I moved to get up off the bed, but I was pushed back down to sit on the bed by the closer of the two men. Much like the situation I found myself in back in Istanbul, my path to the door was blocked by both men. I took in my surroundings and immediately thought about my friends and family. How would anyone be able to find me here in the middle of India if this was to be the end?

Both men were wearing traditional dress: skirt-like attire which also wrapped around their upper chest. The closer of the two men was obviously uncomfortable. His hands were fiddling with the hem of his clothes or more specifically what was beneath his clothes. I was getting more and more uncomfortable myself. The prospect of seeing this guy fiddling with his private parts just a metre or two from me was getting creepy.

The entire scene was like something from the opening of a TV show where the police try and piece together all the events and try to solve a different murder each episode. I wasn't interested in auditioning for the role of "Dead Cyclist" anytime soon, so as soon as they became engrossed in their own argument I bolted for the door. I made it by both men at the first attempt, pushing one of them into the other one to create a bit of time to make it down the stairs, collect my bike and make my escape.

They were lumbering down the stairs like dazed zombies, more from the drugs they'd consumed than the encounter in the bedroom upstairs, as I cycled away down the street. I didn't look back as I hit for the road out of town. The pressure inside was now getting pretty serious. A few kilometres down the road, I spotted a roadside motel just before the next toll plaza and after navigating my way across the busy four lanes of traffic I checked into a room. I was delighted to find the room and the motel more hospitable than what I had just escaped. Before long, I felt relief... and in more ways than one.

35
SEVEN BRIDES
FOR SEVEN
BROTHERS

Four days after checking into the motel, I was finally well enough to check out. I'd been limited to being within a few metres of the bathroom for the entire duration of my stay, although one consequence was that my knowledge of the IPL cricket was now almost as good as any local fan.

I finally reached the Indian east coast and the city of Chennai. I spotted a Subway on the side of the road and as I still didn't trust Indian food, I decided to go with what I knew my body could cope with.

I sat and ate the turkey and chicken sandwich, certain I wasn't going to have a bad reaction to it. My first proper food in days went down perfectly and I was soon back at my bike, unlocking it and preparing to set off when a guy ran over from the ice cream shop next door to the Subway.

"Were you cycling in Goa a few weeks ago?" He asked.

I nodded, and said "Yes."

"At Anjuna Beach, the tree house place, we met there!" the man replied.

It turned out that Shyam had approached me while I was packing up to leave Anjuna Beach. I couldn't remember the specifics of the encounter, but I had a memory that someone had been talking to me as I was setting up for the day across Goa. Obviously, a full bodied, white guy in lycra is more memorable to an Indian guy in India than the other way around.

For the first time in my entire journey I was headed north. Calcutta was still over 1,000 kilometres away.

As I made decent progress up the east coast of India, the heat between noon and two was a continuing problem. Over the next few weeks I passed through cities like Nellore, Machilipatnam, Kakinada, and Visakhapatnam. Each town with a population much larger than most Irish cities, but with names I'd never heard before.

I got another small dose of the runs the morning I woke in Visakhapatnam. After having struggled to find a place to stay the previous night and having had to pay close to normal western prices in the only hotel with availability, I was eager to avoid getting stung for the same again a second night. I knew there was no availability around the city as I'd been to most of the accommodation options the previous evening. They were blocked up for the entire weekend. It was five pm before I had the strength to get on the road, and I set off to find somewhere cheaper to stay. After about thirty kilometres I stopped for what was essentially breakfast for me. I was now feeling a lot better and stronger than earlier in the day. There were accommodation options dotted on the other side of the highway but I knew I had a bit more energy in the tank. I asked the waiter about places to stay further along the road. He mentioned Srikakulam, a city almost a hundred kilometres away.

To avoid looking like a pig headed idiot, I feel I need to explain at this point the way things had been happening up to now. Most

Indians I'd spoken to hadn't travelled much. I'm not talking about to other countries or continents. Many haven't even been to the next town. In my experience, most Indians didn't know where the nearest lodge or hotel was, even if it was as close as a few streets away. The number of times I'd been sent on a wild goose chase by a helpful local when what I was looking for was practically next door was beginning to rack up considerably.

I took the waiter's advice with a pinch of salt. There were at least nine towns across that stretch between dinner and Srikakulam. I'd take my chances that at least one of them would have a lodge or hotel that had escaped the waiter's knowledge.

I got back on the bike in the dark and set off again north east along the main road to Kolkata. I'd charged my phone and lights fully overnight so I was confident the life on the batteries would get me through the night. Luckily, there was a very comfortable and wide shoulder on the highway. I managed to make progress, only being moved by motorbikes, cyclists, pedestrians and animals sauntering in the wrong direction on the side of the road.

I didn't see anywhere to stay in the first town, so I continued through the next two before worry set in. Whenever I stopped at a set of roadside shops, got some snacks and a drink and asked about accommodations, the reply was a little disconcerting. For the third town in a row now, the shopkeeper said "Srikakulam" as he pointed in the general direction of the road.

I realised that it would be well after midnight before I'd find a place to sleep that evening when I came across a police station. One of the officers was sitting outside. I tried to explain my predicament to him, and even asked if it would be possible to spend a night in a cell with the bike. When I was researching my ride I'd read how Mark Beaumont had done exactly that during his crossing of Iran. Unfortunately, my new friend couldn't work out exactly why I wanted a place to stay, and he refused to lock me up for the night.

I weighed up the pros and cons of punching him.

Soon enough, I was back on the road as the thoughts of almost having to explain an assault to an Indian court the following day started to leave my head.

It was after 1 am when I finally reached the town of Srikakulam, the road into the town from the highway was barely 2 kms long, but it felt like 22 as my tired and cold body continued to pedal towards the lights of the city visible ahead in the night sky. I managed to find a hotel but it was all locked up. When the night guard came out, his complete lack of English coupled with my non-existent Hindi resulted in a stalemate. I didn't need to be able to speak to him to establish that I wasn't getting a bed for the night, and besides, there were plenty of hotels visible along that very road.

Eventually an English speaking security guard told me that the following day there were a few weddings in town. A few actually turned out to mean seven. My heart sank. There wasn't likely to be a spare bed in the entire town.

I cycled around the entire town. One hour, and thirteen rejections later, I had admitted defeat. I was beginning to look for a suitable doorway to sleep in for a few hours.

When I found myself back outside the first hotel I'd stopped at, I saw two men waiting to be let in. I started a conversation and explained my predicament, and one of the men offered the spare bed in his room. It didn't take me that long to accept, but as soon as the guard opened the gate to the property, my new friend's companion, who had been banging relentlessly on the door, pulled my friend through and signalled the guard to close the gate, leaving me on the outside. My eye started wandering to the doorsteps again.

A motorcyclist who had driven by moments earlier, probably to see what the banging was about, doubled back, slowed, eventually pulling up right beside me. In perfect English, he asked me if I was ok. I told him I was simply looking for a place to stay and every bed in town was occupied.

"I think that might be partly my fault," the man said, smiling. "One of the seven weddings in town tomorrow is my wedding. All my family and in-laws are in town this evening."

I congratulated him and jokingly suggested I stay with his family.

"If you want to, you can," he said. "We've rented a house for both of our families to stay in this weekend. Follow me."

I jumped on my bike and pedalled as fast as I could to keep him in sight. We stopped at a roundabout where he just sat on his bike for a few minutes. I thought he might be lost or maybe he'd been drunk and I hadn't noticed. The man told me that he was coming from a party and his wife's family were following him in a bus. He was waiting to guide them to the house too.

The bus arrived a few minutes later and, like the strangest procession ever, we made our way across the town. The motorbike leading the bus was followed by my bike and arrived at a home empty of furniture, but with plenty of shelter and security.

After another cold water bucket-and-jug wash, I was assigned the prime location for the night: the spot closest to the single fan in the room. The family and I were lying on mats across the concrete floor of the large open space in the centre of the house. After my appointment as the star guest, the family were located closest to the fan in order of seniority. This meant I was surrounded by the older men of the family, at least one of whom was the worst snorer I've ever heard.

After what felt like less than half an hour, but was probably a few hours, the children were up and running around as the parents and grandparents were still trying to wake up. One of the uncles insisted on bringing me for breakfast as part of the group. I wasn't even hungry. I'd barely slept all night and I just wanted to go back to sleep. My Irish taste buds wouldn't even let me try the offering for breakfast that morning. I was almost at the point of feeling sick. Every time one of the guys took another bite my stomach heaved, so I excused myself and took a few steps out of the tiny roadside shop to wait for them outside.

The family were adamant that I should stay for the wedding that afternoon. A quick mental flick through the clean clothes in my bag quickly reminded me that lycra wasn't suitable attire for any social engagement, never mind a wedding. I really wanted to stay and witness a genuine Indian wedding, especially as the entire family were so hospitable, but as much as I wanted that experience, I knew I needed sleep much more urgently.

I said my goodbyes and was back on the road nice and early. I reached the next town after two hours in the saddle and a motel sign attracted my attention. I needed a place to rest so I planned to get a room for a few hours and hit the road after the mid-day sun had subsided.

The first part of the plan went as I expected, but a few hours later I woke to the sound of banging and crashing. I thought someone was in the room so I flicked the switch for the lights, but nothing happened. The room was still cloaked in the eerie darkness of the storm filled skies coming through the small window high on the far wall. I had no idea how long I'd been asleep or even what time it was. The darkness was everywhere but I could tell I was alone in the room.

The noise, as it turned out, was a storm. Thunder, lightning and extensive rain during the five or six hours I'd been asleep had turned the road outside into a small river. The flash flooding and storms were beginning to get pretty regular now. It was a few weeks before the normal monsoon season but it wasn't unusual to have the storms this early in the year. The power cut wasn't new either. In fact, I couldn't remember a single day in India where I didn't experience a power cut at some point during the day. It had been bad on the west coast, but it was becoming a farce on the eastern seaboard.

Both the storm and the power cut were a constant for the next 36 hours, there wasn't a let up in the weather or an ounce of power until after sundown the following day. Growing up and living in Ireland, being outside in the rain doesn't bother you after a few minutes, but this was different. Torrents of water were flooding from the dark clouds and washing everything along the street outside. It wasn't safe to be outside, so I stayed at the hotel. I knew I was going nowhere until the following morning, but I was thankful to get a rest and catch up on the basic chores like laundry, repacking my bags and planning my route for the next few days.

36
GETTING NOWHERE FAST

I was battling with a dodgy tyre all day as I approached Bhubaneswar. My rear tyre had blown through three tubes today, the last two within a few kilometres of each other. I suspected the cause had nothing to do with the poor road surface on the Indian highway. My tyre wall was shot through. The worn rubber had finally given up, and as I pumped a fresh tube for the fourth time that day, it burst through the side wall of the tyre. I had known I was in trouble but I hoped the tyres would hold up for the last four hundred kilometres to Kolkata.

I could only remember a single bike shop I'd seen in the last month in India that looked like it stocked racing tyres, and I was now beginning to panic about how I was going to continue. I Googled bike shops nearby, but all my searches found me were toy shops or tyres for motor bikes. Unfortunately, road cycling hadn't really caught on across the Indian sub-continent just yet. I wasn't going to be able to progress this evening, and this didn't appear to be a quick fix.

I could see a few hotels and motels advertised on the side

of the highway just a few kilometres ahead of me. The drivers of the rickshaws lined up to my left were gathered around me, half offering assistance, the other half just curious about what might be going on. I pointed at the hotels in the distance and one guy started nodding frantically. He signalled towards one of his colleagues, who pulled up alongside me. Logging the location so I could return there to restart my journey, I set off to find a place to stay and plan my next move.

I contacted Bums on the Saddle, the excellent bike shop back in Bangalore as I suspected they might be able to help me. I was now regretting my penny pinching. When I had been there, I had opted not to replace the tyres when I had the opportunity. I put up a post on social media asking for advice and immediately Dylan, whom I had met in Goa, suggested a few options. He offered to post them out to me from England, but there was no guarantee that they would even reach me here, or how long they might take to be delivered. I was getting desperate.

I took a rickshaw a few kilometres to the city centre where a few of the bike shop locations I'd found on Google had clustered together. After visiting each one of them, with my rear wheel on hand to explain my problem, I wasn't able to find anything close to what I was looking for. A call to Prasad on the other side of the country finally brought some light at the end of the tunnel. He found a bike shop back in Chennai who were willing to ship the parts to me by train and I'd have them within twenty four hours. They just wanted payment before shipping the parts and didn't accept credit card, but Prasad found me their bank details, and I agreed to lodge the money to their account the very next day.

With the evening off, I decided to enjoy being off the bike for once and go for a stroll around the city, soaking up the hectic atmosphere, when I spotted the Holy Grail: a small shop between a bank and a barber shop had a racing bike in the window. I ran over and checked the dimensions of the wheels. They were the exact same as my own, although the tyres were not as good as what I'd been using. I asked the teenaged shop assistant if they had any tyres in the shop, he shook his head. I pointed at the bike in the window and offered to buy the tyres off the display model.

Even though his English was pretty good, the assistant continued to refuse my offer to buy the tyres. He just repeated "Not for sale." I Googled the make and model of the tyres and found out that the pair were for sale in the US for $11. They weren't exactly highest quality, but surely they would be enough to get me the four hundred kilometres to Kolkata and my flight to Bangkok. I offered two or three times the value of the tyres, explaining that they could order new tyres to replace the display ones, but that I was urgently in need of these ones. He asked me to call back in the morning when his boss would be there. I was like a kid at Christmas and practically floated home. The light at the end of the tunnel was growing larger by the hour.

The following morning, I was standing outside the shop when they opened. I had brought my bike as I wanted to check my wheel alignment and get a few other things sorted too. The boss wasn't there, but I asked the shop assistant to call him in my presence. His English wasn't too bad and I managed to explain my situation to him. He finally relented and agreed to give me the two tyres from the display model in the window.

I left the bike with them to get the few bits and pieces that I needed to take care of, but it was going to take most of the day. I cancelled the delivery from Chennai and, at last knowing I was going to be mobile again, decided to treat myself to a cinema ticket and had a very enjoyable date with Spiderman. I picked up my bike and headed back to the hotel to prepare for the next day's ride towards Calcutta.

The next morning I leaped out of bed before I'd even really woken up. My internal organs had declared war with each other once again. Something I'd eaten in the previous few days had decided one bout of Delhi Belly wasn't enough on this trip across India.

As if running to the toilet wasn't bad enough, I barely knew what was coming before I vomited all over the bathroom.

This went on for three days, and so, by the time I got back on my bike and back to the point where I had stopped, nearly a whole week had passed.

I was never so happy to see the back of a city. It had been one setback after another through my entire time in Bhubaneswar. and I was now eager to finish my time in India. The numbers on the signs for Kolkata had changed from ridiculous digits in the multiple thousands to figures I could now get my head around. I had found a flight with a low budget Indian airline IndiGo, who fly to Bangkok. The flight leaving on Saturday evening was perfect for me. I found a little motel about twenty kilometres from the airport that I checked into on the Friday night. The small journey in the morning would be my final mileage in India.

The next morning's ride was closer to two hours than the single hour I'd anticipated, with the heat and detours around the airport each contributing to the delay. I had given myself a few hours to sort out tickets, dismantle my bike, find a box, and pack it for the flight. I needed all that time. On reaching the airport I found the ticket desk and booked my ticket, I was very happy with paying less than $100 for the flight at short notice. It was a good bit lower than the amount I had budgeted for.

Due to the unpredictability of travelling by bicycle, I had made a conscious decision before I started the race not to book flights ahead of time. This decision resulted in paying a little bit over the odds for last minute tickets, but nothing as expensive as replacing a missed flight would have cost me.

My final challenge in India was to find a bike box. I locked the bike up at the airport and set off for a taxi. I explained I wanted to take a taxi to a bike shop, then to a pharmacy, and come back to the airport. I found a taxi driver who knew where there was a bike shop or two. I negotiated a rate for two hours of his time. It took four bike shops until eventually one shop assistant knew what I was talking about. He jumped in the cab with us and directed us to his stores. After going through the stock of new bikes they had there, he pulled one bike out of its box, and sold me the now-empty box at a charge of 200 rupees. It seemed like a king's ransom for him for an empty box, but I was delighted.

When I got back to the airport, I started to dismantle the bike. As with virtually every stop in the country, I was surrounded by inquisitive Indians simply watching as I worked frantically to get my bike ready for travel. Once again, the pedals proved problematic, even with the new spanner I'd brought with me from Istanbul. Finally they loosened and I had the bike in the box ten minutes later. I took advantage of the space in the box and dropped all my heavy items in to reduce the weight of my carry-on luggage.

I checked in and dropped off my bike box. With a few hours to spare to the flight, I found a disabled toilet, locked the door and took advantage of the wet room layout and the small water tap normally used to wash up after taking care of business. The impromptu makeshift shower and change into fresh clothes felt amazing.

I felt like a completely new man as I walked through the security checks. After getting my last Indian meal and waiting for my flight to the next stage of the adventure, it started to sink in that I'd completed another giant step towards finishing this epic challenge.

For some reason, Europe hadn't seemed like such a big deal for me, but being so far from home, and struggling with language, strange food, heat, illness and mechanical failures had made this portion of the trip so much harder. I suspected Thailand, Malaysia and Singapore would be a whole new adventure that I was eager to get my teeth into.

The final call for my flight brought my thoughts back to the present and I handed my boarding card and passport to the smiling Indian girl who waved me onto the plane.

SOUTH EAST ASIA

14ᵗʰ June - 26ᵗʰ July, 2014

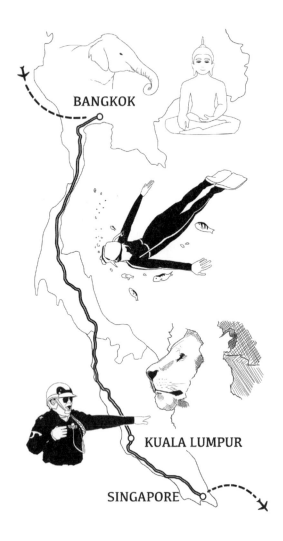

BANGKOK

KUALA LUMPUR

SINGAPORE

Distance: 2,231km
Elevation: 7,793 metres

37
BROKEDOWN PALACE

I landed in Bangkok just a few hours later, and enjoyed the familiar feeling of walking through the airport. I'd been to Bangkok once before, for the World University Games in 2007 and part of my job had been to arrange pick-ups and departures from the airport. I must have come to this airport at least twenty times during that month. I went through my usual routine on arriving in a new country, got a sim card with data for my phone and searched for a place to stay.

I decided to dip my toe in the water by checking out the offers from the guys standing around the terminal building. Compared to the price I'd been paying in the few nice hotels I'd stayed in India, these seemed ridiculous, almost criminally high. I reverted to my tried and tested method of finding a place and opened up the Booking.com app on my phone. Within minutes I had a place to stay for the night just a few kilometres down the road.

I was too tired to even consider building the bike yet so I piled into a cab and got myself to bed. The following morning I tried to make contact with Mark, a friend of a friend of Dylan, who'd offered to help me out with a place to stay. He also was a big cyclist himself and in a professional capacity was the financial director of Spice Roads, the largest cycle touring company in Asia. He told me to meet him at the company, so I built the bike, cycled back to the airport and turned on my tracker.

I eventually found my way to the Spice Roads depot, where Mark and four mechanics were waiting to get their hands on my bike. A new set of tyres, a present from Mark, were matched with new derailleurs, cables, cassette and a chain before I'd left the premises. With four guys working on it, the bike was working as new again within half an hour. Once we'd finished I followed Mark's car back to his house a few blocks away.

That evening, Mark and his youngest daughter, Kara, brought me out to their favourite coffee shop for a sandwich and dessert. It felt great to be having a full conversation with a native English speaker for the first time since I'd met Dylan in Goa, Mark's daughter was also fluent. She had offered her bedroom to me, electing to sleep on the floor of her parents' home.

We went to bed early as England's World Cup fixture from Brazil was kicking off at 5am and Mark wanted to catch the game. I found myself out of bed and on the couch beside Mark watching England take on the Azzurri. The Italians won the game 2-1 and we quickly got our stuff together and hit the road.

Mark showed me the best way out of the city, and we avoided the main roads and dense traffic of the Thai capital. We headed west towards the town of Samut Songkhram, before I planned to turn towards the south and the Thai and Malaysian peninsula that lay ahead of me. A few hours into the ride, I said goodbye to Mark as he turned for home. I pushed on and was feeling really good in the saddle. The few rest days in Bangkok had given my legs a new lease of life.

Over the coming days, I made really good time down the

east coast of the kingdom of Thailand. The beautiful scenery just rolled along under my wheels while the frequent service stops along the side of the road were making me feel like I was spoiled. Each service stop was virtually identical: a 7-Eleven store and the same restaurants and shops in a semi-circle, with a petrol station at the far end. My regular meal had become the toasted ham and cheese sandwich that came heated from the 7-Eleven stores. It was a total lifesaver especially as I didn't need to worry about eating the local food - something I still hadn't quite been brave enough to chance.

One of the main features of the Thailand experience was that each of the small motels or hostels I found to stay in was practically next door to a massage place. The feeling of having someone massage my weary legs and back for an hour or more after a long day in the saddle was only bettered by the bill. It normally cost around five euro and never more than ten.

A few days after leaving Bangkok, I had started the day hoping to reach the city of Chumpon, a decent sized city on the east coast which acted as one of two main gateways to the trio of holiday islands on this side of the country, Koh Samui, Koh Phangan and Koh Tao. Nightfall caught me a little by surprise, slow progress over the hills had meant I'd been caught out after dark once again. Despite my GPS not working, I managed to find my way to the city via a short cut that I had noticed on the map earlier in the day.

I found the cheapest place in town above a small restaurant and although it seemed a little unsafe at first, the other western residents floating around made me feel a little bit more secure. As I ate, I was approached by the staff who, despite having little English, tried to convince me to buy a package holiday to one of the islands.

Even with the language issues, I established that the ferry was just down the road and a bus would pick me up at the door of the hostel. It was ridiculously cheap compared to what you would pay for a similar experience in Europe. As tempting as it was, I knew I had to stay on the road. I had planned a few nights in Phuket in a few days' time and would have to settle for that.

The following morning I set off again, this time headed inland to the hills which separated both sides of the peninsula and, more importantly, the Myanmar border only a few kilometres away. The road from Bangkok had brought me to within a few kilometres of the Myanmar border but with no border crossing, I couldn't add the country to my list. That was going to change shortly.

As I climbed west into the hills headed for the southern border crossing, I couldn't build up excitement about what lay in store. Childhood memories of being cast in a school production of The King & I were mixing with memories of a U2 gig in Dublin where Bono told a story about Aung San Suu Kyi, a politician in Myanmar who had been under house arrest for 15 years for speaking out against the military regime.

All my happy memories of home were wiped out in a split second. A pickup truck which had just passed by in the opposite direction returned to overtake me, then swiftly pulled into the hard shoulder a few metres ahead of me and braked suddenly. I didn't have enough time to swerve to avoid the now-stationary vehicle, and before I could react, I found myself flying through the air. The bicycle, still attached to my feet at the pedals, followed me.

I found myself near the white line in the middle of the road, having been catapulted through the air over the back corner of the truck. The driver of the truck and another two people were out of the car in seconds shouting at me in Thai. It became obvious that they were in fact police officers and they were getting more and more irate.

I picked myself up off the road and moved my bike when the

inner tube in the front wheel exploded. The police all ducked for cover briefly but within seconds, they realised I didn't pose a threat and they were back in my face.

Gestures were being made towards the rear of the truck, highlighting some scratches on the tailgate of the truck. That was when I finally looked at my own wheels. The bike was in bits. One of the brakes and gear shifters had been smashed, only still connected via the cable connected to the bike. The handlebars and the front wheel, which normally lived at perpendicular angles, were now almost parallel to each other. My knees and elbows didn't look much better than the bike and the throbbing pain in my shoulder just wouldn't seem to go away.

Eventually a local woman arrived on the scene. Having a small amount of English, she attempted to act as a translator. She didn't really tell me anything I hadn't already established about the situation. It turned out that I was just outside the police station and the number of police had now grown to about eight, along with a few dozen locals interested in the proceedings.

She told me that the police wanted 4,000 baht, about 50 euro, to fix the damage that they claimed I had caused to the rear of their truck. I remembered advice Mark had given me leaving Bangkok about Thai police and decided to ring him for some advice. He repeated his advice which was: "With Thai police, the foreigner is always wrong. Buy the first guy off, his boss will be more expensive. Protest your innocence but you'll know when to negotiate and pay up."

I found this a little cryptic, but decided he had more experience in these situations so I took his advice, I told the police, through my new translator, that I wasn't paying anything as this was their fault. They couldn't prove the damage was done by me and more importantly I wanted to know who was going to pay for the damage to my bike. This went on for about ten minutes until I spotted the smallest guy going back to the truck, reaching for the glove compartment and pulling out a set of handcuffs.

Mark's words rang in my head and it took me less than fifteen seconds to finalise the negotiations with the one who looked like the boss. I paid 2,000 baht (25 euro) to the police man. They simply handed the money to one of the children who ran away and thencame back moments later with smaller change and they divided it amongst each of the police and the translator in front of my eyes. I was disgusted, but I figured it was a better outcome than being locked up in a Thai jail.

My next problem was how to get myself and the bike back to civilisation. I needed to find a place to stay tonight, have my knee and shoulder looked at and repair my bike. The translator was still floating around and she offered to contact her boyfriend who would bring me and the bike back to Chumpon. I Googled bike shops, not holding out much hope of finding one. I was already planning a train journey to Bangkok to find a solution to the problem, when I struck it lucky. There were a few bike shops in the town, one which was actually a Shimano stockist, the manufacturers of the exact equipment that I had just smashed. And even better, it was across the road from the hostel I'd left barely two hours ago.

My ride arrived and brought me back to the hostel. I booked in and made my way over to the shop. The elderly guy had no English, but he didn't really need any to see the problem. He informed me that it would take three days to get the part in from Bangkok and that I would need to pay a deposit upfront as it was very expensive. I paid the 7,000 baht for the new shifters and I found a doctor who prescribed a course of painkillers and a few days' rest.

Sitting in the hostel's restaurant that evening, cursing my luck, I met an English couple who had just returned from a break on Koh Tao. With three days to wait for the bike and enforced rest from the doctor, I decided to do what any sensible person would, forget about my plans for a rest in Phuket, get out of Chumpon and spend the three days in heaven on a small island in the middle of the ocean.

The island of Koh Tao is a diving and snorkelling paradise, I had no plans for accommodation - I was just taking my chances with the next few days. As the ferry made its way through the dark blue waters towards the quay most of the tourists on board were on the deck taking pictures of this tropical volcanic island with mountains, trees and continuous white sandy beaches. I found myself beside a red haired girl who I had no doubt was Irish. After saying hello, I got chatting to Mary Clarke and her husband Graham, who were on their honeymoon. As we disembarked, they set off for their hotel and we set a meeting point and time for a few hours later to catch up.

I picked a place to stay which looked amazing, but it was located on the other side of the small island. The hotel, built into the cliff face overlooking the ocean, with stairs providing access to an infinity pool and the ocean beneath it, was probably the most scenic place I'd ever been. My apartment had space for four people with two en suite double bedrooms and a balcony overlooking the pool. It cost less than twenty Euros a night. It felt like I'd found a little slice of heaven.

I spent a few hours around the pool and in and out of the sea, chatting to a Korean guy I'd met on the short bus journey from the dock, and it seemed like the fresh air had really taken it out of me. I fell asleep on the bed and woke up in the dark, hours after the time I was supposed to meet my compatriots. I didn't have their contact details to apologise, but on second thoughts, they probably didn't want me tagging along on their honeymoon.

Still lying on the bed, I attempted to get up to make my way to the bathroom but as I moved I realised that I was in pain. I'd obviously burned myself quite badly during the few hours I'd spent outdoors that afternoon. I spent most of the next twenty four hours in the water again, just for the cooling effect on my skin.

On my last day in paradise, I made my way back to the east side of the island where all the activity and shops were located. As I sat eating a meal a few hours before my ferry departed, I spotted Mary with her red hair walking along the beach, hand in hand with her other half. I got their attention, apologised for missing them and they joined me for a meal before leaving the island.

The next morning I picked up my bike and set off. I'd given up on reaching Myanmar, I figured the crash and return to Chumpon meant that something or someone was trying to tell me not to go that way. I'd also already enjoyed the rest and I didn't really have the time to do the same in Phuket. My target was now directly south. I was going to get to Malaysia as quickly as possible.

Over the next few days I made steady progress. The guide-books and the advice given to tourists was to avoid the southern states of Thailand. The areas where Muslims outnumbered the Buddhists seemed to be a hotbed of terrorist activity. With little or no evidence of anything untoward going on, I decided I'd continue along the main road towards the main border crossing into Malaysia. The other alternative, Myanmar, to the west, involved a lot of climbing, and I didn't fancy the long gaps between towns on that route. I'd take my chances with the terrorists.

*   *   *

A few days after leaving Chumpon, I spotted a motel shaped like a pirate ship, and I pulled in and got myself a room. It was during check in as I reached into the front of my bag for my passport that I realised I didn't have it with me.

This wasn't the first time I'd been separated from my passport on this trip. In India I'd left it 100km behind me in the hotel where I'd stayed the previous night. On that occasion one of the staff had jumped on his motorbike and returned it to me inside a few hours for a charge of 400 rupees, or €5.

The prospect of a repeat sent a shiver of dread washing over me. I'd been lucky the last time. This time, I wasn't so confident. I used my driving licence to check into the pirate ship hotel and struggled to explain my predicament to one of the receptionists.

A little while later I was called back by the manager, who spoke much better English. I explained my problem and managed to get the number for the previous hotel. The receptionist immediately recognised my voice and swiftly informed me that I had left without my passport the previous night. He apologised for not having someone return it to my room after they held on to it to be copied for their records, and then explained that it wouldn't be possible for them to release my passport to anyone but me. I would have to come back and collect it myself.

Realising a 200km return trip would cost me two days. I decided it was just easier to go back. By mid-day the following day I was back in possession of my passport.

38

IN THE ARMS
OF THE ANGEL

The border with Malaysia was getting closer. As I made my way south along Route 1, I knew there was only one long day between me and another new country. The day was progressing smoothly enough until after lunch, when I couldn't find a place serving food or drink along the road for what felt like hours. The road signage was advertising a Tesco store but I figured I had fifty kilometres to go to hitting the shop. With the heat, my tired and sore body, and the hilly terrain, it took a lot more than two hours to cover the distance.

As the numbers on the ever more frequent signs dropped to the low single digits, the store appeared to be getting closer but the traffic was beginning to build. At 20kms, I was still too far from Malaysia for it to be tailbacks at border control causing it. As the Tesco signs appeared at the end of a long straight road, it all became clear.

The traffic volume and the constant signage for the last fifty kilometres had been because the store was opening today, in fact the official opening was at six pm, almost exactly the same moment I pulled into the car park.

I took a stroll around the centre but didn't feel comfortable. The strange stares from the thousands of Thai shoppers at the fair skinned, lycra-clad cyclist who was walking between them were really obvious and perhaps even a little intimidating. I found myself a spot in the KFC just inside the front door and after finally getting served I sat down in the corner, and put my back to the front window.

As I normally did in these situations, I took out my phone and opened up my social media account. Immediately a few messages from my sister, Kathy, caught my eye. Two or three missed calls along with a number of messages such as "Ring me ASAP," and "Call me before checking Facebook" were sitting in my inbox. I instantly opened my phone and called her.

In the few moments it took for my phone to connect to the network and for her to answer on the other end, all sorts of horrors were going through my head. I remembered a message from my mother a day or two earlier where she had mentioned that my grandmother was failing and I suspected this was the inevitable news I was calling home for. A few seconds after I connected with Kathy my fears were confirmed. My grandmother had passed away.

It had been just three years since my family had joined my grandmother, the residents of her nursing home and Mary McAleese, then-president of Ireland, to celebrate her hundredth birthday. In reality, she didn't understand what was going on all that much, even back then she had little recollection of who anyone around her was. Even her own children - my mother and her three brothers - all drew blank stares out of her. Nevertheless, she had been the last house call I made before setting off on this adventure, and my trip to visit her occupied most of my last day in Ireland.

My grandmother was a formidable woman, a staunch feminist before that phrase had been coined. Disgusted at the idea of relinquishing her employment as county librarian when she got married (which was a requirement of women's employment at the time), my grandmother re-applied for her position as a married woman. Although she was forced to leave her position, there was no rule forbidding her from returning as a married woman and my grandmother decided to buck the system. Despite protests and objections galore, she was re-appointed to her job, and in the process she changed the outlook for all women working in the Irish civil service.

Childhood memories flooded back into my head of the many happy encounters we'd had over the years as my sister's voice brought my thoughts back into focus.

"What are you going to do?" Kathy asked.

I'd spoken with my mother about the possibility of something like this happening, and we'd decided that I'd only cut my trip short for a death in the immediate family. There were too many people committed to supporting my efforts and the message I was trying to spread to spend valuable time, energy and money on travelling home to a funeral where I'd already said my goodbyes in person during her life.

"I'm going to keep going, I think she'd want that," I replied.

It felt like only a few minutes later when I looked at the half-eaten KFC meal in front of me. The steam which had been rising off it was now long gone. I picked a few more bites but didn't have the stomach for it. Instead, I wrote down everything that was in my head about the passing of my grandmother. Twenty minutes later I had written a long-winded account of what she meant to me and posted it to my social media pages. I found myself openly crying in the corner of the restaurant as I was typing.

I must have looked funny to the locals: a white guy in his mid-thirties, clad entirely in lycra, with a cold unfinished meal in front of him, as he sobbed into his phone. I just didn't care.

It was dark when I left, but I set my sights on reaching the border. I already knew I would take tomorrow off to get my head together.

I followed my standard routine. Fasten my backpack, swing one foot over the back of the saddle, stand over the bike and place the ear phone in my left ear, and leave the right earbud speaker hanging through my helmet strap. This allowed me to hear passing and approaching traffic while being able to distract myself with a song, audio book or podcast. This time around I hit shuffle on my iPhone playlist. With over one thousand songs on my playlist, my phone started playing Sarah McLachlan's haunting 'Angel', which had my eyes welling up again. By the time the chorus rolled around, I was on the road alone thousands of miles from home, but I felt like I'd just picked up a passenger for the remainder of my journey.

39
TERROR IN THE SKY

After a few days off to get my head together I crossed the border into Malaysia. I planned to get to Penang that evening. My daily distances were dropping, and I was conscious that I was starting to lose time. My finishing time didn't matter that much anymore. It had been a few weeks since Lee, the sole remaining competitor in the race, had been disqualified for breaching the rules when he rode in a taxi for a 200km section in India.

The race directors had not agreed with his interpretation of the rules and when he didn't rectify his mistake they had no choice but to disqualify him from the race.

With no upper limit on completing the event, all I had to do to win was stay within the rules of the race, and finish it.

Knowing I had the race title secure allowed me the freedom to take my time, and enjoy the people and places I encountered along the way. The turtle had been given an opportunity to beat the hare, and this turtle intended to take full advantage.

* * *

As I made my way through the Malaysian countryside, I couldn't help but focus on the jungle along the side of the road, with all the animals under the sun visibly enjoying life at the tops of the trees and in the darkness underneath. Monkeys were a daily sight. Shapes on the road that looked like twigs or branches turned out to be lizards and snakes, a fact which often enough startled me much more than my approach seemed to surprise them.

I was beginning to struggle with the heat and the hilly terrain in Malaysia was proving to be even more draining than I had anticipated. I passed through the state of Penang and the small towns and villages I ended up in proved to be hospitable and friendly. Small motels and hostels, although slightly more expensive than they were in Thailand, were of a much higher quality and it felt good to be comfortable and get some proper rest again.

The night before my push into Kuala Lumpur, I found a small motel just off the main road. It was still ridiculously early to sleep, so I turned on the television. An English language station was broadcasting a show featuring cool and trendy things to do in Malaysia. One of the first reports was on a brand new café in Kuala Lumpur where they had married a love of coffee, food and bicycles into one location called 'The Grumpy Cyclist'. I decided that café would be my first port of call in the capital the next night.

Armed with a new destination, I set off towards the city in the morning. As the road got busier, wider, and scarier, I swapped the main highway for smaller parallel roads and some bike paths I found along the way. Eventually, the main road became the only option I could find through the mountains to the north of Kuala Lumpur. As night fell I pulled into a petrol station and caught a glimpse of the city's skyline for the first time. The Petronas Twin Towers stood in front of me, providing a simple visual reminder of the exotic location that I had cycled to. It really began to sink in that I had made it to the other end of the planet on my own steam.

I set the GPS to guide me to the café, and after another hour or two, I found it. It almost felt like home. I grabbed a table outside and ordered a steak. The smell indicated I wouldn't be disappointed, and by the time I'd taken the first bite I knew I wasn't going to be a grumpy cyclist this evening.

I introduced myself to Aaron, the bike mechanic, and he dropped everything to come and have a chat about my journey. He then brought over a few of his friends so that they could also hear my story first hand. I had a lovely evening in the company of Adli, Kashfi, and Sim. When I said that I intended to visit the towers the following day, I was slightly surprised to find that none of the people around the table had ever been there. We made a decision that we would go together the following day. I was going to bring the natives to show them their own city. I left my bike with Aaron and made my way to a small hotel I'd found online just a few streets over.

The next morning Adli & Kashfi collected me and we made our way into the heart of the city, and then to the foot of the towers. They were some of the most impressive buildings I'd ever seen in person. I got a little bit of a shock when I went to pay for my ticket. My two new Malaysian friends were charged a fraction of the cost I had paid to get in, an obvious nod to the economic spending power of the average Malay citizen compared to the normal tourist.

The observation desk and the walkway between the two towers was amazing. The 360 degree panoramic view of the city nestled in a small basin between hills on all sides was beautiful. The museum dedicated to the largest skyscrapers ever built was very informative, but as I looked out over the city, I couldn't help but be drawn to the imposing hills to the south that I knew I would face the next day.

I ate lunch at an Irish bar in the courtyard at the foot of the towers. It was your typical cliché Irish bar, in that it was exactly like every other Irish bar around the world, but not at all like any bar that existed in Ireland. As I ordered water and browsed the menu, I asked the guys what they were eating. "We're fasting. It's Ramadan," they replied, shaking their heads.

My knowledge of the Muslim faith is limited, but the boys explained that for the month of Ramadan, nothing could pass their lips from sun rise to sun down each day. They enjoyed a breakfast in the pre-dawn darkness and then feasted each evening as the darkness enveloped them again. No food or drink was permitted. I felt bad consuming food in front of them, but as they explained they had prepared for the day with a hearty breakfast and while it was their religious belief, they respected that it wasn't mine.

We hung out in the city for a little while before making our way back to my hotel, promising to meet up at the café that evening. I had agreed to participate in the café's normal Thursday group ride. When I arrived, Aaron had stripped my bike down completely, totally de-greased all the individual parts and rebuilt it. When I went to pay for his work, he wouldn't let me. We set off with twelve brave souls through the built up streets of Kuala Lumpur. As far as enjoyable rides go, it wasn't one of my highlights, despite the great company. There was barely any open road, and we had to be very vigilant sharing the road with heavy car traffic. Little over an hour later, we found ourselves back in the café for dinner. Aaron introduced me to the cafe owner, Alex, who had insisted on supporting my ride by not charging for the bike service.

We talked about everything, especially the chances of me seeing the only TV exposure they had gotten since they opened a few months earlier. Suddenly, the buzzing atmosphere in the café dampened down and everyone went quiet. It was as if the school bully had just walked into a classroom. It didn't take long before I discovered why. People started checking their phones, whispers flying between and around the tables dotted throughout the cafe.

"It's happened again, another one's down."

"Excuse me, I need to call my sister, she's a flight attendant."

As people in all corners of the room stopped talking and started to focus on their phones, I turned to Adli and asked what was happening.

He diverted attention from his phone. "Another Malaysian plane is down. This time it's been blown up over Ukraine," he whispered.

Everyone was frantically trying to check the status of their loved ones. Some managed to contact their flight attendant siblings or their pilot cousins from the café and establish that they were safe, but the fear remained on the few faces left in the room about other friends who might have been involved. It seemed everyone knew plenty of people who might have been on that flight.

I made my way back to the hotel in an eerie silence. The streets were quieter than they had been just hours ago, and the staff in the hotel were nowhere to be seen as I made my way up to the room. Starting out the following day, the hangover from the incident was well and truly evident. All the newspapers carried the crashed plane on the front page. All the flags in the country were flying at half mast. As I made my way to the south traffic was noticeably lighter. It felt like I had gate-crashed the largest funeral I'd ever been at.

Speaking of funerals, I'd just missed my grandmother's at home a few days earlier, and she was still in my thoughts. She'd been laid to rest alongside her husband, who had predeceased her by almost fifty years, in a grave near her parents' in the village of

Fenagh in County Leitrim.

On the map of Malaysia I'd been following since crossing into the country, I'd been drawn to a word on the page since I'd first looked at it. Fifty kilometres to the south west of Kuala Lumpur lay Carey Island or Palau Carey. I did a bit of research and found there was a nice restaurant at the end of the Island so decided my way of having my own little nod to my grandmother would be to take a small detour and have lunch there.

I found the restaurant without any difficulty. It was part of a very exclusive golf resort, but as it was Ramadan they didn't have any food available until after sundown. The hotel and resort were out of this world and I knew I was going to struggle to pay for dinner, let alone stay there. My only problem now was that I was starving and it was another thirty kilometres ride back to the nearest shop. I resigned myself to a few hours of gazing at the rubber plantations that stretched along the road as far as the eye could see.

As I made my way back towards the door of the hotel and my bike I spotted a special offers poster promising a two night package for two people including meals for less than the cost of a single night's stay. It didn't make much sense, and it was still outside of my price range, but it was worth a try. I approached the front desk, and explained my situation.

I was cycling around the world, my grandmother whose maiden name was Carey had just died, and I was trying to spend a night on Carey Island in her memory. After some crafty negotiation I was left with a room in the lap of luxury. I had completely blown my daily budget, but it just felt right.

Top: **Grand Designs - the breathtaking views of the Grand Canyon**

Centre left: **Straight & Narrow - Cycling one of the longest portions of perfectly straight road in the world in the Nullarbor Desert**

Centre right: **Petronas Towers, Kuala Lumpur**

Bottom: **Sydney Opera House & Harbour Bridge**

Top: On Stride - Taking part in the Boyne 10km during Challenge Ten

Centre: Rugby Riders - My first bike tour in New Zealand in 2011

Left: Marathon Monday - The gang setting off for Dublin City Marathon 2011

Centre left: The Thurles Ten - The brave souls who joined me when the main cycle was cancelled. (l-r) Sean Nolan, Padraig Cullen, Nora Kleen, Christy Bannon, Martin Carroll, me, Alistair McDermott, Ben Condell, Darryl Johnston & Brian Condon

Opposite centre: Rebuilding - Putting the bike back together in Belfast

Inset above: Burned Out - My cycling shoes falling apart after 30,000 km

Inset below: Not Quite Home - Dublin, South Australia is a little smaller than its namesake

Top: Starters Orders - Leaving Leitrim to cycle around the world

Bottom: VO2 Max - Getting put through my paces by Sean Kinane

Top: Fully Loaded - I certainly packed light on my trip

Bottom left: Storm in a Hot Tub - Making the most of the thunder and lightning in Fargo, North Dakota

Bottom right: Misfit - Sharing the message "It's OK not to be OK"

Top: Dune du Pilat: Sand dunes towering over the French forest

Centre left: One of the many last minute accommodation finds

Centre right: Katrina: This view from my couchsurfing hosts in Bay St. Louis featured six houses before Hurricane Katrina

Bottom: Sea Staring - Taking it all in at Lucky Bay, Western Australia

Clockwise from top left:

Super Swede - I met Martin on the French west coast

Shamrock Send Off - Leaving Guardamar del Segura for the final portion of the ride

Hero of the Game - Being introduced to the crowd before a MLS game in Boston

Welcome Home - Family and friends waiting at Dublin Airport (right/left)

The Big Apple - Invited to speak at Consulate General of Ireland, NYC

Grizzly Adams - Before and after a shave

Bottom left: Finish line, London

Centre: Family Ties - (l-r) Ruth, Dad, me, Mum, Matthew, Kathy & Charlie

40
GROUNDHOG DAY

With five days to spare before my Australian flight I found myself in Simpang Renggam, a day's ride from Singapore. As I browsed through the accommodation options online I was considering staying north of the border in Johor Bahru until the day of the flight to take advantage of the cheaper cost of living there, when suddenly the face of Grainne, an old college friend, popped up on my Facebook page and she invited me to stay with her and her husband Richard and their three month old son Paddy in Singapore. I couldn't accept her offer quickly enough. Grainne would be the first familiar face I'd seen since leaving my sister in Austria almost five months ago.

An early start helped, but progress was slow on account of a pair of flat tyres, having to find replacement spare tubes, and struggling with the heat. By the time I was supposed to meet Grainne, I hadn't even entered Singapore. It took almost another ninety minutes to cross the border. The lack of a quick pass and the novelty of seeing a cyclist seemed to trigger every possible issue the border guards could have had. At one point, I looked like I wouldn't even be let into the country. They finally saw sense and I crossed the causeway that joins Malaysia to Singapore.

Singapore boasts an interesting record. Once part of Malaysia, Singapore remains the only country in the world which was granted its independence against its will. The country had been kicked out of Malaysia by the Kuala Lumpur government back in the 1960s.

I faced a decision whether to stay on the highway which would take me right across the country or drop onto the lower back roads and take my chances with no route map or directions. I opted to drop off the road but within a few hundred metres that road re-joined the highway, leaving me with no option but to hit the hard shoulder of the main artery of the city state. Nicely tucked away from the traffic in the hard shoulder, I made fantastic progress, although the occasional blast from a car horn was a bit of a distraction. I suspected that I really shouldn't be there and as I passed another off and on ramp I regretted not taking advantage of the opportunity to get off the road.

I prepared to slow down and pick my spot to cross the slip ramp when a car slowed right down and roared at me in English that I shouldn't be on the road. I was beginning to agree with him. As I made my way the three kilometres to the next opportunity to get off the road I was absolutely flying down a hill when I felt the bike shudder beneath me. I looked down and saw the debris of a car crash beneath my tyres. Tiny shards of glass littered the ground, and within a few seconds both of my tyres gave up the ghost. I scoured my backpack and found my final two tubes to replace the burst ones. I was going to need a large amount of good fortune to not pick up another puncture today.

Eventually, I made my way into the city centre, found a McDonalds to get the free Wi-Fi, but it turns out that's not a thing in Singapore. I managed to get a basic map and worked out directions before finally getting Wi-Fi from a local hotel. I found my way to within a few blocks of Grainne and Richard's apartment before finding some more Wi-Fi to check my messages. There were a few messages from Grainne asking if I was ok, but luckily the offer to stay with them was still good. Grainne gave me directions and I found their house within a few minutes. After a shower, we sat and chatted for a while. Richard and Grainne had a late night barbecue on their balcony and I slept like a baby in their spare room until late the following morning.

Although I was within a stone's throw of the airport, I hadn't yet reached the end of this leg of the trip. Richard was enjoying a day off and he joined me in finishing off the Asian leg of the cycle: a ten kilometre spin through local parks and the southern coast of the island, before we found ourselves on the highway which was the only point of access we could find to the airport. As we reached the welcome to the airport sign, we took the obligatory photograph at the airport and turned to head back to the apartment.

Crossing the road and heading away from the airport caught us some unwanted attention. As we reached the first off ramp and prepared to leave the fast flowing traffic a policeman ushered us to the side. He was particularly ignorant and wasn't interested in hearing about why we were on the road. Once he established I was a tourist, he focused on Richard and took his details. as if he would get bonus points for snaring himself an expat victim.

I took advantage of the few days off to catch up with Grainne and got to know Richard and Paddy. On the Sunday morning they dropped me and the bike the short distance down the road to the airport. Despite my protests, they insisted on waiting with me until I'd checked in. It turned out that was a good idea. I had mixed my dates up and arrived at the airport a full day before my flight.

I had to spend another day in Singapore. Grainne and Richard had been invited to a barbecue that evening and they brought me along to meet some of their expat friends. It was fantastic to have some semblance of normality for an evening, although I knew with Australia, New Zealand and the USA as the next few countries on my list this would become a little more normal for me. The following day we went back to the airport, and as I boarded my flight to Perth, Western Australia, my mind raced with terrifying thoughts of snakes, insects and the vast, unoccupied, Nullarbor desert I would soon traverse.

AUSTRALIA

4th August - 29th October, 2014

PERTH

NORSEMAN

CEDUNA

ADELAIDE

MELBOURNE

SYDNEY

Distance: 5,752km
Elevation: 32,159 metres

41
SNATCH

On leaving the airport in Perth, I was surprised by the cold and by how dark it was at 6:30pm. I purchased a local sim card and got my communications up and running. I had made plans to stay with Alan Taylor, the boyfriend of Shauna, one my neighbours and friends at home in Leitrim. I rebuilt my bicycle on the curb outside the airport terminal, drawing strange looks from one of the staff.

I think beyond the curiosity of what exactly I was up to, he was wondering about my box and the other bits of cardboard that were scattered around me. I think he feared he'd be left with the job of cleaning it all up. I took pity on him and made sure I left no mess for him to clean up as I went along.

I eventually found my way into the city and through to the district of Como on the east shore of the Swan River. Alan was home alone in a house he shared with a number of other Irish people. They all worked on the mines or railways in the north of the state and simply used the house as a location to stay in the city between contracts. When I stayed there, most of the rooms were empty, but by the time Alan served up a steaming plate of steak with potatoes and vegetables, it felt like I'd landed home in Ireland.

I spent a few days around Perth. I think partially because I was enjoying the novelty of being in an English-speaking country, and also because there was a huge Irish population in the city. I caught up with Daniel, an old school friend I hadn't seen in years, grabbed a drink with Neil and his girlfriend Alicia, hung out with Una and even caught a Gaelic Football game that some friends were playing in. I really enjoyed the few days of rest and recovery. My bike also underwent a full service with a complete overhaul of its setup that would make life a little easier across the next few weeks. I had been dreading the isolation that would come from the intimidating distances I was going to be covering with no one around me for hundreds of kilometres.

I added Tri-Bars to the bike, as well as extra water bottles beneath the seat in place of one of my bags. I packed up my bulky stuff in a box which I left with Alan so he could post it later to wherever I was going to end up staying in Adelaide. The lighter setup was fantastic. Less weight meant being able to go slightly quicker, which allowed me to pick up the pace and comfortably cover a larger distance each day. This made it slightly easier to plan my route, with my average distance now coming much closer to the two hundred kilometres a day I had originally planned for.

As I was preparing to leave Perth, Colin had put me in touch with a lady in Bunbury who offered to have me stay with her family. After an early start, I was on an excellent bike path that took me well out of the city. Going against the flow of traffic of the bike commuters heading to work, I noticed the houses and estates becoming less and less dense, and then less and less common, until

I crossed the brow of a ridge and suddenly saw nothing but the road stretching into the distance as far as the eye could see. It was a sight I was going to be getting exceptionally familiar with over the coming weeks.

Approaching three hours into the day I was starting to get hungry and knew that Mandurah was coming up ahead. I finally found a small shopping area with a Hungry Jacks, the Australian version of Burger King, near the entrance to the car park, I ordered breakfast. I was the only person in the premises, and so I jumped up to go to the bathroom, leaving my things behind me on the table I'd eaten at. I covered my phone and battery pack with a newspaper as they sat on the table charging.

Less than a minute later, I emerged from the toilet, and was almost knocked over by a bulky teenager who pushed his way past me towards the door. I had a bad feeling, and as I looked over at my table I saw the newspaper was sitting flat, and there was no evidence of the phone and battery pack underneath. I asked the clerk if he'd seen anyone near my table and he pointed at the guy who'd just left saying, "I think he was in that area."

I ran out of the restaurant and to the corner of the building to see the youth had already ambled halfway across the car park. I let out a roar in his direction and he stopped, turned around and waited for me to make my way over to him.

His first mistake.

As I approached the youth, I guessed that he was somewhere around sixteen or seventeen, definitely not old enough to be out of school on a Monday morning. He seemed a little bit surprised that I'd followed him. As I got closer I realised this guy was huge. I didn't fancy my chances against him in a physical challenge. I was going to have to try a different tactic.

"I'm really sorry to bother you, but my phone has gone missing from the table in the restaurant. One of the staff said that someone who fitted your description was in the area around my table and I thought maybe you might have seen something or even someone take it from the table?" I said.

The young man seemed confused. I'm pretty certain that wasn't the opener he was expecting. He shook his head from side to side slowly and told me that he denied all knowledge. His tracksuit bottoms showed a rectangular shape in a pocket while his left jacket pocket also showed the outline of a phone. I suspected he was still hiding this morning's ill-gotten gains.

"Would you mind showing me what's in that pocket, it looks like a phone," I said, pointing at his left jacket pocket.

He immediately whipped out a phone, showing it to me while saying, "This is my phone." It wasn't mine.

His second mistake.

The youth's tone and body language confirmed what I already suspected: that he had my phone, and that it was elsewhere on his person. I pointed at what looked like a cigarette box in his tracksuit bottoms pocket and he duly removed the packet and displayed them to me.

"Would you please mind emptying each of your pockets so that I don't suspect you took my phone?" I asked.

He started to feel his way around his body, checking and emptying each pocket of their contents, except for the pocket I suspected held my phone. I stood my ground and waited for his face to look even guiltier, before asking, "Is there any particular reason why you won't show me what's in that pocket?"

"That's just my other phone!" He croaked as he pulled my phone out, with its distinctively smashed back facing towards me. I could see the staff of the restaurant all lined up against the front window over his shoulder. They were watching the encounter, but did not even attempt to help. Wordlessly, I reached out and took back my phone.

"How about you give me everything else back too, you walk out of the car park, I'll head back to the restaurant and I don't report this to the police or even the restaurant," I said.

Within ten seconds all my belongings were back in my possession and he shuffled away out of the middle of the road. I hastily made my way back to the restaurant, packed my things, got on the bike and high-tailed it out of town. It had been a long day.

That evening I stayed with Chantelle, Garry and their boys Scott and Rhys at their house just south of Bunbury. Chantelle was a fantastic host. She called her colleagues and friends around the state and further afield to set me up with places to stay. Pauline in Adelaide was happy to have me and sent me on her address in order for Alan to forward my belongings. David in Margaret River and Cathie in Esperance were also now waiting for my arrival.

I followed the main road as far as Busselton, where a flat tyre took a little bit of wind out of my sails. I managed to find a bike shop where I could inflate my tyre properly. The hand pump I'd brought with me was merely a stop gap until getting a proper foot pump. Once back on the road I made the journey to Margaret River, a town famous for its wines. It was also well-known to my family. My mother had lived and worked there for a period on her travels between graduation and settling down. After checking in with David at Prideau's of Margaret River, he invited me up to his family home for dinner, an offer I gladly accepted.

After coming back to the hotel, I wandered around the corner to the only business open on the main street, a pub which was showing the Ireland and New Zealand game in the Women's Rugby World Cup. It was strangely comforting to sit at the counter watching the Irish girls beating the Kiwis, with myself and the Australian barmaid shouting at the television almost in unison: I was supporting the Irish; she was cheering against New Zealand. I was enjoying this, so I decided on taking the longer, quieter, and more scenic route to the south west corner of Australia at Leeuwin Lighthouse near the small town of Augusta before I'd turn towards Pemberton, over one hundred and twenty kilometres along the only road heading east.

A few days later, I found myself in Albany, the quiet seaside town and the home of Cathie and her daughter, who offered me a bed for two nights and an opportunity to go whale watching in one of her friends' charter boats. Twelve of us went into the open Southern Ocean, and all seemed fine until suddenly the water turned nasty. By the time it calmed down half of us, including me, were hanging our heads over the side, being sick.

Cathie had organised an interview with Owen, from a local Albany newspaper. Towards the end of the interview, Owen asked me how the news of the suicide of Robin Williams made me feel. I was stunned. One of my favourite performers and a massive cycling enthusiast had chosen to cut his own life short. I didn't know how to respond. I had planned to eat breakfast on the way out of town, but as I sat looking at my pancakes, I realised I had no stomach for the journey ahead. It was two hundred kilometres to Jerramungup, with only a small settlement about half way at Wellstead to break the journey, I just didn't think I had it in me. The pancakes were still sitting on the plate, but all I could think about was the news that Robin Williams, who I think was the funniest man on the planet, had taken his own life. If the perennial joker and funny guy couldn't see a reason to stay alive, what was I trying to do? Was it a fool's errand? Was I kidding myself that I was making any difference at all to anyone?

I didn't have the heart to get back in the saddle that day. My focus was gone. I just wanted to go back to bed and pull the covers over my head for twenty four hours and fight again tomorrow. I didn't have the heart to go back to Cathie's, and so I started to investigate the youth hostel in the town, when all of a sudden

Cathie texted me. When she realised I hadn't left town, she insisted I stay with her another night.

I didn't have the stomach for any debate at the moment, so I found myself back on the bike and outside her back door within a few minutes. I did exactly what I thought I would. I went back to bed and slept. I wasn't sure what the next day would hold. Would I give up on everything and just call it a day, book a flight and fly home, or would I keep going? I really didn't know.

42

FANTASTIC BEASTS AND WHERE TO FIND THEM

I left Albany the following morning, but progress was slow. There was no accommodation in the town of Wellstead along the way, but the local shop keeper, Dawn, took pity on me. She offered a room in her own home. Her husband Rick brought me on a little tour of the area, and took me right down to the beach and the kangaroo sanctuary nearby.

A couple of days later I reached Ravensthorpe just before sundown and, after getting directions from the pretty girl in the petrol station I joined the normal Friday night football crowd in the local pub, where I also managed to snag a bedroom for the night.

When I woke up in the morning, something told me to stay in town. I couldn't quite put my finger on the feeling, but a look at the time at eight am and knowing I faced almost two hundred kilometres to Esperance was enough to indicate to me that I wasn't going anywhere today. I wandered over to the petrol station for a morning snack and got to chatting with Chloe, the pretty girl behind the counter.

As I left the shop I saw a motorbike pull up, fully branded with slogans and information about "The Black Dog Ride." I knew the black dog was used as a description for depression so I approached the two riders and quizzed them on their reasons for being here.

I quickly discovered that Sam and Vanessa were participating in a round-Australia motorcycle ride with dozens more bikes. They were the first group of the day, but the remainder would be through town later, including Steve Andrews, the founder of the ride. Steve had originally done the ride around the entire continent of Australia on his own in 2009 to raise funds for suicide prevention. We chatted for a few minutes until he had to get back on his two wheels and lead the team on to Esperance and beyond.

I was facing into a long day in the saddle on my way to Esperance, so I planned to eat early and get a good rest before starting off the following morning. I had just ordered my dinner in the pub when in walked Chloe, the girl from the store. Things were looking up.

Chloe's entrance was darkened for me somewhat when a guy followed her in. We were the only people in the restaurant portion of the pub, and although we were at opposite ends of the room, the guy was so loud it was impossible not to eavesdrop on every word he said. It became clear pretty quickly that they weren't a couple and, despite his best efforts, that wasn't going to change anytime soon. When I finished eating I returned to the main section of the pub. Only three spare seats were left along the wooden bar. I sat in the first one and within five minutes she was in the seat beside me, with the guy taking up the final place on the other side of her.

He eventually went for a cigarette. He hadn't even left the bar before I said, "Chloe. From the shop, right?" Just like that, we started chatting. Her 'date' came back a few times over the next few hours, eventually offering to walk her home, but she declined instead asking me to walk her the short distance back to her house. I duly obliged, and even grabbed a sneaky kiss along the way.

As I made my way back to my room after leaving Chloe's home, I couldn't stop smiling. It might have just been a kiss, but after two years of my life without even a second glance from a girl, I was over the moon. The girl who had caught my attention on entering town had ended up returning the interest that I'd shown her.

It was with newfound enthusiasm that I set off for Esperance. This was the first real test of what was to come daily along the Nullarbor Desert. There was nothing between the two towns except nearly one hundred and ninety kilometres of road. No water. No food stops. No resting places. This was to be my first real experience of how I was going to feel for two whole weeks.

I realised almost half way into the day that I didn't have my SPOT tracker with me, and it was too late in the day to turn around and get it. I decided to keep going and get them to send it on to me at Norseman. It got dark long before I reached Esperance. I knew I was facing into a long night ahead in the dark. I took a picture of my Garmin indicating almost one hundred and thirty kilometres already covered in front of an all-too-familiar road sign saying "E 60," meaning there was another sixty kilometres to Esperance.

In the late dusk, the photo was blurry and unclear but I'd found myself in a rare spot of phone coverage, so I posted it to Facebook. The result was both unexpected and amazing. My phone screen lit up in the darkness from where I had mounted it on the dashboard area I'd created around my handlebars and tri bars. Comments and likes from home and from supporters around the world would pop up sporadically, and each time light started emitting from the phone's screen it was as if someone had just rolled alongside me in the darkness to help me along the road.

It might not have seemed like a massive effort to the people just clicking 'like' on social media, but the effect on me was great. Those little bursts of light had the effect of passing me their energy, seeing names and profile pictures appear on the notifications as I cycled along through the dark night, trying to avoid the road trains which had become huge bundles of light and noise through the pitch black sky.

As the road signs counted down in five kilometre bursts, I was beginning to get worried about whether I'd manage to survive the road trains which were passing me faster and closer. My flashing rear light was the only thing keeping me from becoming roadkill. I finally reached the town of Esperance and found the hostel along the shore. The gentle lapping of the waves in the darkness to the right hand side of the road indicated I was going to be in for a visual treat when I got up. I needed to get my bike serviced ahead of my assault on the Nullarbor Desert and finalise my decisions about what equipment would be coming with me and what I would leave behind.

I was facing into the first of my two biggest fears since signing up for the World Cycle Race. The second was the Rocky Mountains, but they were still in my future. The Nullarbor Desert, a stretch of over 1,200 kms, lay ahead of me to the east with no towns or villages across the entire stretch of road between Norseman in Western Australia until Ceduna in South Australia.

There would be nothing but vast numbers of potentially deadly animals, snakes, and insects, and maybe some more approachable ones such as kangaroos, camels and wombats.

Even the name of the place struck fear into my heart. A direct translation from the Latin "Nullarbor" gives us the English phrase 'No Trees'. That's before you even get to the desert bit. As the translation would suggest, the majority of landscape would be nothing taller than ankle or shin height, just low scrub as far as the eye can see. The mostly-flat horizon would be in plain view at all times, and in all directions. The complete lack of water and food was to prove to be my biggest concern with only a roadhouse every one hundred and fifty kilometres on average. A roadhouse consists of a petrol station, a small shop, a restaurant, a bar and a half dozen or so motel rooms. The entire operation would fit into a decent sized country home in Ireland and is managed by a staff of between six and ten people who live on site.

In Esperance, I found a sports shop with a great bike mechanic who replaced some parts on my bike that were looking a little worn. I got a new chain with a new hanger for my rear derailleur, and I was looking forward to getting going again. I used my day off to join two girls from the hostel in a sightseeing day in nearby Cape Le Grand National Park where the white sand beaches are separated from each other by the iconic granite shoreline.

On our way out of the park, I spotted something moving ahead on the road.

"Stop!" I roared.

Nadine, who was driving, slammed on the brakes in the middle of the empty road.

"What?" she asked, as she could see nothing ahead of her.

I pointed to the middle of the road, where what appeared to be a dark stick lay motionless. Then it moved and started to slide across the road.

"It's a snake," I said, as I grabbed my camera and jumped out of the car.

I approached the snake with the camera, careful to leave enough space between me and the serpent as it moved off the roasting hot surface towards the brush at the edge of the road.

Another guy approached from a car headed in the opposite direction which had stopped, and we all just took in the sights.

It was only when we got back to the hostel and compared the video footage from the encounter earlier that day with the poster of "Ten Deadliest Things in Western Australia" hanging on the wall that we realised we had come within a few feet of a Western Tiger Snake. An untreated bite from this venomous creature has a 40-60% mortality rate.

Upon reaching Norseman the following evening, I found myself in something that resembled an old American western town. Dusty roads, with the streets practically empty it looked like the land that time forgot. Norseman was an old mining town which had ceased working relatively recently. The people left when the jobs and money did. It painted a very bleak, but real, picture of the enormous inland portions of the Australian continent. I found the hostel I'd booked a room in, and it was almost a replica of the town in a single building.

The decrepit and run down hostel appeared totally deserted and I had to call the landlady to let me in, and the inside of the building was bitterly cold. I had to sprint through the freezing corridors to use the showers at the end of the building, and the warmth started to come back into my body only after I tucked myself under the covers.

The next day, after leaving the hostel in Norseman, I grabbed breakfast at the petrol station at the main junction in the town, sitting under the road sign which read "Adelaide 1986". It felt a little daunting, and I genuinely wasn't sure if I was going to be able to make the entire distance. Concerns about the bike or my body breaking down were beginning to creep back into my mind, but I pushed my doubts to the back of my mind, tightened the strap on my helmet and swung my leg over the cross bar of the bike. As I pushed off from the step I took a few deep breaths and let my legs kick back into doing what they did best.

43
INTO THE GREAT WIDE OPEN

Less than two kilometres into my day, I made the decision, after careful consideration, to ride on the wrong side of the road. Until now, the shoulderless roads gave me barely four or five seconds notice of traffic coming up behind me. There were too many close calls when I became aware of a passing vehicle when the sound of the engine came into my earshot. My warning time was cut even shorter when I was listening to music.

On the wrong side of the road, however, I could rely on my eyesight picking the trucks, camper vans and cars from a few kilometres away. This gave me more than enough time to evaluate whether traffic was coming from behind me and to revert to the correct side of the road long before anything dangerous came from either direction. In the rare case of a road train coming from both directions, I just pulled off the road and waited for both vehicles to pass me before continuing my journey.

Night one in the Nullarbor was spent in the surprise find of Frazer's Range. I was feeling wrecked after a day in the heat and crossing the rolling hills coming out of Norseman, and even though it was early in the day, the thought of committing fully to another four hour ride to get to Balladonia didn't seem like the best option. I decided a wiser plan was to drop anchor in Frazer Range and start nice and early the next day.

The farm house at Frazer Range was small, but it sat on a rather large portion of land: half a million acres to be exact. It was a distance of more than 160km from one side of the farm to the other, making its 2,000 sq. kms just marginally smaller than the size of the average Irish county. And yet, Frazer Range was not big enough to make the top one hundred biggest farms in Australia. The Irish half of the lovely couple running the station gave me a room for half price on account of my accent and the bike. I joined the other residents for dinner later that night in the small restaurant on site.

The next day, I made my way to Balladonia. There wasn't even a single turn off the road that could have set me wrong. That experience would become common for my days traversing an absolutely barren wilderness. After hours and hours in the saddle, I'd have seen nothing. Not buildings, not towns, nor trees or even hills to break the view to the horizon. Next was the 90 mile straight, an almost never ending, unadulterated straight portion of blacktop which led to the next roadhouse at Caiguna.

After Caiguna, the roadhouses at Cocklebiddy, Madura, Mundrabilla and Eucla all provided lodgings for the next few nights as I approached the state border with South Australia. It is forbidden to carry foodstuffs across the South Australia border crossing along the Eyre Highway, which posed a major problem for me, as I was carrying supplies that were meant to last the remainder of the 200 km journey towards Nullarbor Roadhouse. Luckily, the roadhouse at Border Village allowed me to restock on some fruit and water, although the cost was, as usual along the

Eyre Highway, ridiculously high. Here, a two-litre bottle of water cost between five and six dollars. A night's accommodation at one of the roadhouses didn't offer much change from 120 dollars. I needed to get out of this part of the world as soon as possible. With the heat, the cost and the sheer distance between water and food sources I was struggling to cope.

Thankfully, the tailwind that joined me for the first day in South Australia carried me the two hundred kilometres to the Nullarbor Roadhouse. When I went to pay for the room at the roadhouse, my card was declined. I'd been expecting this to happen for some time now and was a little surprised that it hadn't happened up to now. I found myself hundreds of kilometres away from any form of civilisation and over a thousand kilometres in either direction from anyone I actually knew.

I logged into my PayPal account only to discover it was bone dry. I managed to convince the manager of the roadhouse to give me a bed, and told him that I'd settle up the following morning. I had to leave my passport as security. I was beginning to wonder how I might get myself out of this mess.

I knew my regular monthly payment was due from FIT Magazine in two days. I'd also been selected as a potential sponsorship recipient by Version 1, a Dublin-based software company. Their quarterly programme allowed their staff to nominate projects to receive financial support. I'd need every penny of it, but that cheque was a few weeks away at the earliest. I called home, and my Mother offered to send me the money I needed to survive until my pay cheque came.

At the next stop, Nundroo, I got chatting with Rob and Brennan Price over dinner. They were a father and son duo from Ceduna who were working mid-week near the roadhouse. They offered me a bed in Ceduna, and the following night I settled into the comfy mattress in their home.

The next few days saw me relax and spend some time with the Prices as they showed me around the lovely, if quaint, town of Ceduna. I'd been dreaming of civilisation for the two weeks it took me to cross the desert and I was enjoying just being around buildings, people and not having to pay two or three times the normal price to enjoy a meal.

44
THE LONG AND WINDING ROAD

I set off south into the Eyre Peninsula and landed in the town of Streaky Bay. About five kilometres outside the town, I was passed by a cavalcade of motorbikes. The first one took me by surprise, but after ten minutes of watching bikes passing me, I had almost become accustomed to the roar of the engines on the road. When I pulled into the petrol station in the town to get my bearings, the motor bikes were all around me.

I was approached by Lacey, one of the organisers of the ride. When she heard about my adventures, she invited me to join the group for a meal. The Police Commissioner's Fund for Sick Kids, also known as 'Bright Blue' was the charity the ride was supporting, and most of the motorcyclists were police from Western Australia. I was introduced to the police commissioner himself during the course of the evening and towards the end of the night I fell into a small group gathered around a table. I was asked about my journey and the reasons behind it.

As I told my story, I was asked by Maureen, an Irish girl working for the charity in Perth, how I funded it, so I started explaining about the different sources of funding and how people had been giving me support, via crowdfunding, along the way. Terry, who had barely said a word all night, turned to me.

"How can I help you? I'd like to donate $2,000," he said.

I started laughing, thinking he was joking. The looks on the faces of the girls on the other side of the table indicated he wasn't. Terry asked for my bank details and when he found out I didn't have an Australian bank account he handed me his phone and his credit card. "Get it to the point I just have to press okay." Converting currencies for the crowdfunding page, it fell to just over 1,400 Euro so he insisted I round it up to an even 1,500 Euro.

I was totally shell-shocked. Between my wages (now in the bank!), this contribution, and the impending sponsorship, I would have enough to get me through the Southern Hemisphere.

I stayed in some interesting places over the coming weeks, including the rural, isolated, village of Lock in the middle of the Eyre Peninsula; a room overlooking the old bank in Snowtown, famous for the Snowtown Murders; and with the teachers of a high school at which I was invited to speak, in Port Augusta.

As I approached Adelaide, the bike was beginning to show the signs of the wear and tear I'd put it through across the desert. The chain was slipping through the gears, one or two spokes had snapped, and some groaning noises were now coming from the bike. I decided to stop at Dublin for the night. I pulled off the highway only to realise that in South Australia, Dublin was tiny. The town was little more than a petrol station and a pub, and there wasn't a single bed available, so I set off for Two Wells. Soon after darkness fell, I punctured a tube at Lower Light, a small village along the highway.

A passing motorist stopped and offered me a ride to the pub. I was too tired to refuse. After a warm meal and a good night's sleep, I fixed the bike. Thalia, one of the girls working in the pub, drove me the ten kilometres back to Lower Light.

Passing through Dublin the previous day had piqued my interest about the legacy of Irish settlement in Australia, and after a quick Google search I found a Leitrim Street in Salisbury on the north east of Adelaide, which I decided to visit on the way to the Robinson's house in Adelaide. I spent three days charging my batteries with Pauline and Mathew and getting my repairs sorted in a local shop.

The road to Melbourne proved to be highly interesting. I watched locals street brawling at closing time in Murray Bridge, spent a day on Ronald and Belinda's sheep farm at Coonalpyn, visited the Blue Lake in Mount Gambier and stayed with my friends Maureen and Leon Clarke in Keith, whom I'd first met at Nullarbor Roadhouse, and then again at a petrol station near Port Pirie two weeks later.

Eventually, I reached the start of the Great Ocean Road. I spotted a cyclist stopped ahead of me on the side of the road. He was laden down with panniers, and I stopped to make sure he was okay. Will van Rompaey had suffered a puncture but was just about to get back on the road, so we joined forces. From Melbourne, he had decided to tour the world-famous tourist route on his week off. He and his brother, following in a support car, were planning to stay in a hostel in Port Campbell that night. I was invited to gate crash.

When we arrived, the hostel was closed. Thankfully, we managed to find the manager of the motel nearby and convince her to allow us to stay there. The hassle was well worth it. The view out over the port and the beach outside was a great sight to wake up to the following morning. Will and I were feeling tired after the late night, so we decided to soak up the beauty of the seaside town.

After a relaxing day off, we decided to head for Apollo Bay, on the other side of the Great Otway National Park. We went for a quiet game of pool that evening when four English girls walked into the bar, and our quiet plans for the night ended up scuppered. The girls eventually prepared to leave around 3am, but just before that one of the girls decided she'd had enough. She went by herself towards the caravan park they were staying in.

Ten minutes after leaving us, the remaining three girls came back to look for their lost friend. In her slightly drunken state her friends were worried that she might have ended up in the ocean just across the road from the hostel.

Luckily, Will and I had decent torches and head lights, so we split up into three pairs and set off looking for her. Will made for the beach while I went with one of the other girls to double check the route back to the caravan park, searching in bushes and drains along the way.

When we didn't find her along the way, I suggested that she might have wandered home and just missed the others along the way. When we got back to the caravan park, we discovered her sleeping in her own bed. Disaster averted.

45

ON THE ROAD AGAIN

When I was crossing one of the long stretches along the Nullarbor, a car pulled in a few hundred metres ahead of me and waited for me to catch up. This didn't happen often, but Rick and Amanda Kehoe insisted on me taking a can of coke, some biscuits and fruit and a few litres of water to restock my supplies. We swapped details and arranged to meet when I got closer to them in Lorne.

As I made my way along the Great Ocean Road, I got a message from Rick on Facebook inviting me to stay with them. I couldn't refuse. Earlier in the day, Will and I had met two Spanish cyclists, Maria and Zigor heading the same way as we approached the seaside town. We had joined with them to create a little convoy. We pulled into the car park overlooking the golden beach and started to eat lunch. I was a few hours early for Rick and Amanda, and I didn't want to upset their plans by arriving early. As we were sitting there, Rick happened to pull up beside us in his car. He'd decided to take a little trip out the road to see if he could spot us on the outskirts of the town.

Rick extended the invite to the Spanish couple and suggested we keep cycling towards the next town, Anglesea, telling us that he or Amanda would follow us later, find us a place for our bikes, collect us, give us a place to stay and drop us back at our bikes the following day. It seemed too good to be true, but we didn't need to be asked twice. Rick left us to our lunch, and as we finished up I spotted a familiar-looking man with red hair walking up from the beach. Because he was wearing a distinctive pair of Gaelic football shorts, my first instinct was to assume he was Irish, that was until he bounced and caught the oval Aussie Rules football he'd been carrying like he'd been doing it all his life. I turned my attention back to the group around the picnic table. Suddenly, I heard a voice behind me.

"Breifne, is that you?"

I spun to see Aidan Reynolds, a brother of Sharon, an old school friend, walking towards the table. The red hair and the Gaelic football shorts suddenly brought a smile to my face as I put two and two together. I hadn't seen Aidan in ages because he was now living in Melbourne. His parents followed him up from the beach and we spent a few minutes shooting the breeze before they continued on their road trip.

Amanda met the three of us in Anglesea armed with a hamper of food and a fridge of cold drinks. We stored the bikes in a local surf shop and travelled for an hour back to their amazing house in what proved to be a beautiful town. This visit was one of the highlights of the Great Ocean Road. We cycled to Geelong where the Spanish couple caught a train into the city. Thanks to the rules of the race, I didn't have that luxury.

In Anglesea, I spent a few minutes looking for the small caravan park in Geelong that I had stayed in with 60 of my college friends on a college sports tour back in 2001.

September 11th 2001, to be exact. On the evening of the

11th, I remembered sitting with two of the tour organisers as we watched the live pictures of the second plane hitting the twin towers instead of prepping for a media interview the following day. It took a few minutes for the enormity of the event to sink in with most of the group, buoyed by the alcohol and the frivolity that had just ended abruptly.

The absolute panic that set in when the first tower fell was matched when the second came down. A few members of the group had family and friends in New York and there was a scramble to get into the town to find a pay phone to call home for news in the midst of our terror and panic. In the end, everyone's loved ones were safe, but some had very close calls. Needless to say, our interview didn't happen the following day.

It was a long day before I got into Melbourne, but in the small town of Lara I found my way onto the Capital City Bike Trail, which took me right through the city, past the bustling nightlife of an after-work Friday evening in the state capital. Cycling along the crowded river banks as people dined, drank and socialised was a really nice experience. It had been a while since I'd witnessed the hustle and bustle of a city like this first-hand.

The route took me over the Jim Stynes Bridge, where I stopped briefly to pay my respects. Stynes was a Dubliner who had become a local hero in Melbourne. After a very brief Gaelic football career in Ireland he decided to try his luck with a professional game and became a legend with the Melbourne Demons, becoming the first and only non-Australian born player to win the prestigious Brownlow medal awarded to the best player in the league. He eventually became the club president - a position he held until his untimely death at the hands of cancer in 2012.

My friend Síle lived at the other side of the park, in Richmond, and I received a lovely warm welcome in her home. It felt fantastic to be able to relax and spend some time catching up with her and her boyfriend Michael.

I spent a couple of days catching up with other friends around the city: Caitrin for a drink one evening, a stereotypical Australian barbecue on the beach with Caz and Mairead, and a brunch with Andrew and Claire. It didn't take long for the restlessness to creep in. I was concerned that I was eating too much; that I was pushing my luck with Síle and Michael's hospitality; and, perhaps most importantly, that I was in danger of being stuck in the country past my ever-closing 90-day tourist visa. I needed to get back on the bike and head for Sydney.

A few days later, after passing through Moe, Sale, Longford and the very scenic Lakes Entrance, I arrived in Orbost. I'd been offered a bed by a lovely vicar, Rowena, who lived there. Her two other guests were Sarah and Coline, two French girls who were travelling around the country. After I arrived to Orbost and found the house, I spent the whole evening swapping travel stories with Rowena and the French girls.

The next morning, Rowena talked me out of getting back on the road. She was taking the girls into the mountains to nearby Buchan. A day strolling in the mountains with pretty French ladies sounded way more appealing than getting back in the saddle. It was. Not only did I get to spend more time with the girls, I also got to meet fellow cyclists, Kane and Stephen, who travelled with me as far as Eden.

I met with Ellen and her parents, Stan and Karen, whom I'd been in touch with through the Couchsurfing app. Ellen convinced me to take my first roller coaster ride, and Stan gave me the guided tour of the beautiful seaside town and helped me with my visa concerns.

I'd entered Australia on a 90 day visa, and it was very close to expiring. By this point, I had four days to leave the country and was facing into a very quick final sprint to Sydney and international departures. Stan rang a friend in the immigration department, who told us that a visa extension application would cost over $350 and wouldn't be guaranteed to succeed.

"What happens if I don't leave the country within the ninety days?" I asked.

"If you're longer than 28 days overdue, you might be deported and may be banned from the country for two years," Stan's friend replied.

The punishment didn't seem all that bad. I had no plans to return to the country within the next two years and I guessed I only needed a few extra days to complete the ride as planned.

I decided to take my chances at the immigration office at the airport, having faith that my Irish accent would be the perfect tool to get around any issues with officialdom in Australia.

Some of the places I stayed over the next few days were incredible, and the Sea Cliff Bridge was one of the highlights. I'd been looking forward to this since it had been mentioned to me a few towns back, because the road just shoots out over the cliff before turning back down along the lower face of the cliff. With the Pacific Ocean on my right and the cliff wall a few metres to the left, it was without a doubt one of the most amazing stretches of road I'd experienced so far. The best part about the phenomenal view was that I was going downhill, so I simply allowed gravity to do its job while I enjoyed the view.

As the night crept in, I finally found my way around the coast of Botany Bay to Sydney Airport and completed this leg of the trip. I took a few days with a former colleague, Deirdre, in Sydney and caught up with friends, then got my bike boxed up and ready to fly, and had my now-traditional post-continent shave and haircut.

I was ready to leave Australia, albeit a little later than I'd initially intended. At the airport, I was stopped at security and sent to speak to a member of the immigration team, who gave me a very short and unintimidating dressing-down about how I shouldn't have stayed so long. With a smile and a nod I was through, and Queenstown bound. I could almost taste the Fergburger already.

NEW ZEALAND

5th November - 12th December, 2014

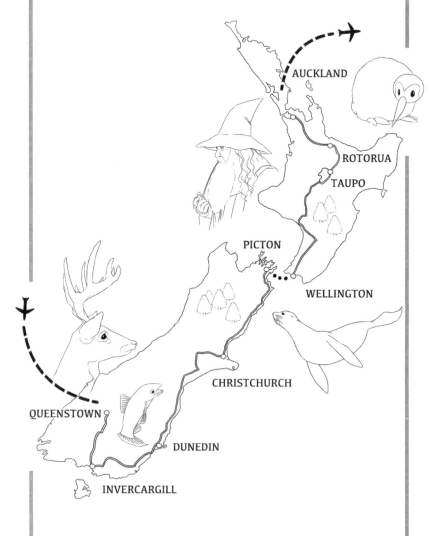

AUCKLAND

ROTORUA

TAUPO

PICTON

WELLINGTON

CHRISTCHURCH

QUEENSTOWN

DUNEDIN

INVERCARGILL

Distance: 1,968km

Elevation: 15,299 metres

46
THE
NEW ZEALAND
STORY

The approach into Queenstown was horrific. As the small airplane was thrown around the sky over the Crown Range Mountains, I had two main concerns: first, that the turbulence would result in me getting to review my breakfast choices; and second, that the plane wouldn't make it over the mountains.

As I buried my face inside the sick bag, I looked out the window to see the Crown Range road emerge below me. It brought horrific memories of the day I spent climbing the mountains three years earlier as part of my first cycle touring experience, raising funds to look after paralysed rugby players back in Ireland. Thankfully, the view also brought back the happy memory of descending thirty kilometres of mountain road into the zigzag switchbacks that brought the road down to the base of the mountain at Arrow Junction.

Before I knew it, we were on the ground. I was very excited to get to the Base Hostel because it was just across the road from my favourite burger joint on the planet: Fergburger. The next few weeks promised to be very exciting. In addition to continuing the race, I would be catching up with many old friends. Better yet, my financial concerns had been eased somewhat. Base Backpackers Hostels had kindly offered to support my journey by offering me accommodation in each of the cities that they had a place, so I already had lodgings arranged in Queenstown, Taupo, Rotorua and Auckland.

With friends and other contacts offering beds in some of the other towns along my route, I was confident I could keep the costs down. Then a minor miracle happened when a Facebook group dedicated to the Irish living in New Zealand put out an ask for help, which met with overwhelming support.

I took a couple of days in Queenstown to let my hair down and enjoy the atmosphere. I decided to treat myself to a slap up meal and ordered the steak and ribs combo in one of the Irish bars in town. It was Melbourne Cup day and slowly as the race drew closer the bar started to get busier. I got chatting to a group of guys who had sat beside me named Drew, Garry and Ronnie. When they heard what I was doing in town they started firing questions at me.

When it came time to settle my bill, Drew insisted on paying for it. I felt bad, as for once I'd decided to actually get a nice, and therefore expensive, meal. I was a little embarrassed, but karma repaid Drew's kindness when the horse he'd backed took the cup, landing him a payday ten times what my meal had cost him.

The next day, I left the adventure activity capital of the world and headed along 40kms of the narrow road named The Devil's Staircase, wedged between the east shore of Lake Wakatipu and the jagged slopes of The Remarkables mountain range before I ended up in the town of Lumsden. I had arranged to meet Miriam Bielski, a girl from Meath who was now married and living here, who had seen the post on Facebook.

When I pulled into the town, I saw three happy smiling faces running towards me when I got off the bike. Seamus, Quilan and Saoirse got to me a little bit before their mum and had told me all the arrangements for the evening when I finally got to meet her. The kids were a bundle of energy, and they helped me forget about my sore legs after the long day in the saddle.

I was convinced to spend an extra day when I reached Invercargill, the self-proclaimed 'Arsehole of the World'. Keith Richards or Mick Jagger had called the town that back in 1965 and the locals kept the insult as a slogan for the last fifty years. Fearghal and Sarah had offered a place to stay there but it happened to clash with the arrival of Sarah's cousin Jillian and her boyfriend Nick.

I ended up on the couch, but I thoroughly enjoyed the company of the two couples for the day I stayed with them, and when Jillian heard I was headed for North America, she volunteered a bed in the Los Angeles area.

The next few days would see me head for Dunedin, passing through Gore and along the presidential highway to Clinton. Of all the strange things I saw along the road, this opportunity of naming the stretch of road between the two towns who shared the name of the US president and his vice president was one of the best. After Clinton, Balclutha and Milton, I found myself on the outskirts of Dunedin and eventually found Greg and Suzi's home in the hills overlooking the city. Greg was a childhood friend of my cousin Alan. As a pair, they introduced me to *Star Wars* when I was nine years old. They'd been issued with babysitting duties they figured a midnight showing of Darth Vader and Luke Skywalker would fit the bill. They were right.

* * *

I'd been to Dunedin before, three years earlier, and I hadn't thought much of the city. This time, I'd found a different, much nicer, side to it. I spent a day discovering the Catlins Forest Park with couch-surfing Canadian cyclist Lisa, her brother Tom, and their parents.

I moved on from Dunedin, but not before I took a small detour on the way out of town to the bottom of Baldwin Street. Sometimes it's hard to say which end of a street is the top or bottom, but there was no doubt here. With its thirty five degree gradient, Baldwin Street is officially the world's steepest street. I found myself staring up at the little platform-like space at the top of the rise. Two cars tried it and just about made it, coughing and spluttering their way up the steep climb.

As I stood, holding my bike, at the intersection with the main road, I had this feeling that I'd regret it forever if I didn't at least attempt to go up on the bike. What's another 300m after 16,500 kilometres, right? As I turned into the street, a yell of "Good Luck" from an American couple made me realise that I was about to become a spectacle. A group of Japanese tourists started clapping and cheering as I reached the start of the serious climbing.

I made it about one third of the way up before realising I was carrying too much weight. I discarded my bags and unneeded equipment from the bike and set off again. I got about half way up before I had to work my way back and forth across the road in a zigzag to progress. It took over eleven minutes to reach the top of the road, but I felt better than I had in years when I got to the top and looked back at the drop. If I could cycle up the steepest street in the world I would never again be scared of any climb, no matter how steep.

I passed through the towns of Palmerston and Timaru before staying with Caroline and her family in Ashburton.

The family of rugby pundit Brent Pope lived two doors down. Pope was a kiwi who was a fantastic advocate for mental health promotion back in his adopted home in Ireland. Caroline's parents wanted to bring me over to say hello but I said no. I'd seen Brent Pope on TV, but I didn't know him at all, and I didn't want to embarrass myself by showing up on his parent's front step.

I decided to take a route through Methven to reach Christchurch so I could see Rakaia Gorge. The Rakaia River is just an hour's drive outside of Christchurch, but it feels like it's on another planet. The glacial melt waters in the river flow down from Mt Hutt in the Southern Alps towards the Canterbury plains, and the blue hues cast out by the river as it passes through the narrow canyon are nothing short of spectacular. The approach to the century-old bridge across the river is a long downhill stretch with the river roaring through the canyon far below the left hand side of the road.

I had to stop just to take it all in before continuing on to Christchurch, where I stayed at Darren and Eri's home that evening. Darren had taken the next day off to show me around the city, it was startling. I'd been in Christchurch in the immediate aftermath of the earthquakes three years earlier and it had been heartbreaking to see the old beautiful buildings lie in partial ruin. This time around, the city had a different energy: full of hope and possibility in light of the opportunity to redraw the map for the area and redesign the city centre.

The mixture of the emptiness of the old city area and the rebuilding going on everywhere was truly inspiring, and the atmosphere was one that promised a bright future for the historic city. I could see a lot of similarity between the directions of my own life and that of this city in the last four years. Almost devastated by events outside our control, we were both redesigning our futures in a positive way.

I spent that afternoon helping Darren build a deck. We were cutting back trees, measuring the spaces, buying the wood and cutting it to the lengths required. I'm not usually one for DIY but I really enjoyed getting my hands dirty. I think the best part was being able to help out a little around the house and not just take advantage of the free place to stay.

Later, in town, Darren and I met my friend Gemma for lunch. Gemma had been one of my original fifty blind dates in the original Challenge Ten list. We'd stayed in touch and meet up from time to time, so with Darren back at work, I ended up hanging out with Gemma for most of the few days in the city. Rachel, a friend of a friend, had invited me to a birthday party, even though I'd never met anyone who would be there. Gemma agreed to come along in case the whole experience would prove to be a total disaster. We ended up having a really great night, and by the end of it I wasn't too happy about leaving her behind.

I had mixed feelings as I packed up my stuff and set off north again towards the ferry port at Picton. In particular, I struggled to get Gemma out of my mind. It was only after a horrible day battling against ridiculous tailwinds that I found my way to the tiny village of Waipara. I arrived at Waipara Sleepers; a hostel made out of disused railway carriages, and grabbed the last bed in the place. That was when I discovered there was a birthday party going on. Warren and his friends had missed his milestone birthday a few months before, and they were making up for it now. I got invited to join the group for their party and they even fed me from their ample supply of food. It was a good thing as there wasn't anywhere open at this hour. All the local shops were already closed.

I spotted her when I went into the kitchen. The flame-red curly hair was the first thing that struck me. I instantly assumed she was Irish, but it turned out Eva was actually a German living in Switzerland, currently driving around New Zealand as part of a world tour. We exchanged pleasantries and I made my way back to the party. When I got back to the dorm half an hour later, I was pleasantly surprised to find Eva was sharing my dorm.

She was chatting to an Argentinean guy when I arrived but within half an hour, his lack of English or maybe just his shyness saw him quit the conversation and he made his way to his own railway carriage for sleep. Eva and I just seemed to click straight away, conversation was flowing and before long I found myself kissing her.

The next morning, I woke up reluctantly, knowing I was headed north east to Kaikoura and Eva was headed towards Christchurch, in the opposite direction. She had left the dorm before I'd woken up and when I wandered out for breakfast she was getting ready to leave. She'd even taken the time to write me a note before she drove off. She made me promise not to read it until after she'd left the hostel. My mind was racing. Less than 24 hours ago, I couldn't get Gemma out of my mind, and now Eva was flying around my head. My only choice was to get back in the saddle and let the road take all my focus and attention. It almost worked.

I stayed in another hostel in Kaikoura, one that had been designed and laid out just like the houses in Hobbiton, the hobbit village in Lord of the Rings. The entire country had decided to cash in on the profile and success of the film trilogy and nearly everything had a *Lord of the Rings* twist.

The ride to Blenheim was fantastic. I stopped to check out the sea lion sanctuary just outside Kaikoura, and I spent some time chatting to a guy who emerged from the water clad head to toe in diving equipment. He'd been diving for abalone, a form of sea snail that is an expensive delicacy.

As anyone who's travelled through New Zealand quickly learns, most journeys involve going up and over more mountains. On my final push into Blenheim, darkness threatened to make my descent horrific. In addition, road works had reduced the road to a single lane with stop / go lights.

As I set off through the lights, the truck behind me decided not to force his way past me. This meant all the traffic going up the mountain pass behind the truck had to travel at the speed of a slow-climbing cyclist. Luckily, no one seemed too put out by the delay, and I even received a few friendly horn beeps and waves.

I'd been put in touch with a Monaghan woman, Sinead McKenna, who ran a hostel in Blenheim and the vibe on arrival was great. Sinead had kept me a dinner from the barbecue they'd had earlier in the evening. I showered and joined the gang for a drink. Sinead's brother Sean and his crew were taking the same ferry as me to the North Island so we decided that once I'd cycled to Picton Port the following morning I'd load the bike into one of the cars and save myself the price of bringing the bike on the ferry. Our ruse worked: I was asked to pay for my own passage, but my bike got to cross for free.

47
ON RAGLAN ROAD

After we landed on the north island, The Monaghan crew and I agreed to meet up later. They headed on to National Park Village, while I stayed for a few days in windy Wellington with Sarah, a classmate from university, to help celebrate her birthday. I also caught up with another former member of the 50 dates club, Niamh, who had now moved to the New Zealand capital. Niamh suggested I stay an extra day and registered me for the Wellington Beach Gaelic Football 5-a-Side competition.

As a child growing up in Ireland, nearly everyone plays Gaelic football. I didn't realise that playing the game on a beach in November was even on my bucket list until I'd actually taken part in it. I was recognised by Marie, a neighbour of sorts from home who had been following my progress on Facebook. She invited me to her bar for breakfast on my way out of town the following morning.

After a whirlwind of excitement in Wellington, I set off over the mountains towards Palmerston North, taking the coast route through Paraparaumu. By the time I got there, I considered calling it a day, as my legs were sore from the previous day's beach football games and the climbing that morning. Unfortunately, I was expected in Palmerston North. An old colleague Sandra and her husband lived there and had offered a bed. Thoughts of home started to run through my mind as I approached the town of Shannon, surely named after Ireland's longest river, which winds its way through my home town.

Sandra and JD were excellent hosts. I even got invited to play with JD's football team. Buoyed by my decent showing in the Gaelic, I agreed. I managed to last maybe six minutes of puffing and panting around the pitch before I volunteered for goals. It turns out bike fit doesn't necessarily translate into football fit. As a badminton coach, Sandra insisted that I join in her club's coaching session too. It had been nearly fifteen years since I had played the sport but I signed up willingly, excited about lengthening my break from the saddle.

It was in Palmerston North that I experienced the scariest moment of the entire trip. That evening after the football game is one I'll never forget. Sandra and JD had planned a meal with their friends Sujay & Cathy and Bruce & Leonne but when Cathy had to take her baby, Garreth, to the hospital, Sandra had been recruited to mind their other son, 2 year old Liam. We ordered Thai takeaway after the hospital checkup, and I joined the three couples in Cathy's front room. Then, there was chaos. The baby started to suffer a fit, turned purple, and stopped breathing. Cathy was amazing, she immediately kicked into protective mother mode and gave mouth-to-mouth and chest compressions to her son while Sujay spoke to the ambulance operator and JD and I kept Liam occupied on the other side of the room. After the ambulance arrived and whisked the mother and baby away for further tests, the five of us remaining simply sat around the room in shock, only too aware that the situation could have ended tragically.

A few days later, after a painful couple of days climbing into the highlands of the Tongariro National Park, Sean had kindly organised a room for me in the Park Hotel Ruapehu where he and his girlfriend Nikita worked. I sank into the hot tub there and enjoyed the relaxing and soothing feeling of the hot water on my tired and sore muscles.

The next day, I had been invited to take on the Tongariro Alpine Crossing but I was highly underprepared for it. With no decent hiking shoes or even long trousers I couldn't consider it. The day itself had ridiculously bad weather, so it was probably the wisest and safest call. I spent the next few days cycling through the terrain made famous by the *Lord of the Rings* movies. Mount Ngauruhoe, made famous as Mount Doom in the Hollywood films, was one of my personal highlights.

The Base backpacker hostels in Taupo and Rotorua offered me a place to stay as I made my way north around Lake Taupo. I visited my friend Nollaig and her husband Josh in Raglan before I set off towards the largest city in the country. I soon discovered not only that my wheel needed to be repaired, but also that my brakes had stopped working. It took a lot longer than expected to get my bike sorted, which put me under pressure to reach Auckland by nightfall. The heavens opened as I stopped for dinner about ninety minutes from Auckland. There were two other cyclists there, a Japanese couple, and they had no intention of going back out in the rain.

The Japanese couple told me there was a train to Auckland from just around the corner. I had a few days to kill before my flight and knew I could come back and complete the distance the next day. I jumped on the train with them, stayed dry, and came back the following day to complete the journey to Auckland Airport.

I had misjudged how long it would take me to reach Auckland. This meant I found myself with the best part of a week to spend there. I caught up with a few friends around the city. Aidan, the boss who had head-hunted me for GrabOne, met me for breakfast one morning and Nick picked my brain for his own cycle adventure home to Scotland over a meal one evening.

The packing was the easiest it had been so far. Less than a kilometre from the terminal at the airport was Natural High, the bike rental company owned by my friend Andy. Andy offered to service my bike before I left. His staff even boxed the bike up and dropped me and the bike to the nearby terminal.

I couldn't have asked for a better-send off. It was a perfect end to an amazing six weeks in Aotearoa, the land of the long white cloud.

USA

18th December, 2014 - 13th April, 2015

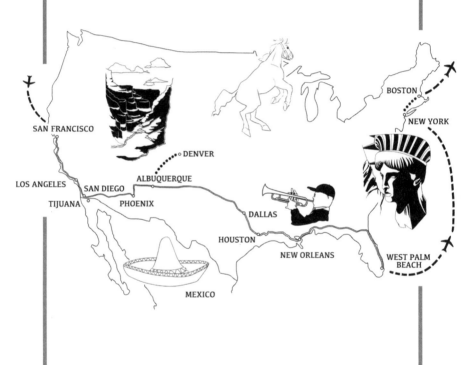

SAN FRANCISCO

LOS ANGELES

SAN DIEGO

TIJUANA

PHOENIX

DENVER

ALBUQUERQUE

DALLAS

HOUSTON

NEW ORLEANS

MEXICO

BOSTON

NEW YORK

WEST PALM BEACH

Distance: 6,061km
Elevation: 33,164 metres

48
BACK TO
THE FUTURE

Before I set off on this adventure, I got my hands on a copy of the original *Around The World in 80 Days*. I read the classic story, full of anticipation about visiting a number of these locations myself, and had forgotten about the end of the story. Phileas Fogg returns to London a few hours after the 80 day deadline has passed. His servant realises that he has got the date wrong and he's actually a day earlier than he thought.

Landing in San Francisco was my first experience of time travel. After a twelve-hour flight, I had landed in the United States a full eight and half hours before I'd taken off in Auckland, thanks to having crossed the International Date Line. For me, December 18th 2016 was 45 hours long.

In the airport, I found a designated space with a bike stand and tools, and rebuilt the bike properly before heading north along the bay towards the city. My friend Hugh Gibbons had offered me a place to crash in the city. His address on Lombard Street seemed familiar, but it was only when I came to the top of one of the hills that the city by the bay is famous for and looked at the curved road snaking its way down the other side that I remembered why. Having chosen the safe option and walked down the steepest street in the world back in Dunedin, this time I decided to take the plunge. I made my way gradually down the iconic street with the brakes fully engaged for nearly the entire distance down, whilst leaning back into the saddle to avoid tipping over the handlebars.

I had been invited to speak to a gathering of staff in a nearby communications company the next day, and my friend Conchubhair showed me around, introduced me to the group, and then helped me record a new video to promote my crowdfunding campaign leading up to Christmas. On Saturday morning, Hugh rented a bike, and we cycled across the iconic Golden Gate Bridge to go to Sausalito, where we were joined by Liana, Hugh's other half, for breakfast in a restaurant with a view of Angel Island, Alcatraz, Fisherman's Wharf and the fog-covered bridge.

We took the ferry back to the city. As the Golden Gate Bridge emerged from the fog, I recalled that it was not only the most photographed structure in the United States but also the location with the highest suicide rate. I allowed myself a moment to say a little prayer that my entire cycling endeavour would result in just one single person not making that decision in the future.

The next morning found me back in the saddle and headed towards Santa Cruz. I had been invited to spend Christmas with Jillian and her family in Orange, just south of Los Angeles, but it was too far to make it in time. I was looking at spending the holiday in the saddle until Laura, an Irish girl who had been following my journey, invited me to Sacramento for the holidays. I left the bike in Santa Cruz and hopped on a bus to San Jose where I met Laura's friends Bob and Jamie, who were driving the four hours to Sacramento. The next few days were awesome, especially Christmas Eve in an Irish Bar with Laura, her sister Courtney and friend Jeremy singing karaoke, followed by Christmas day in Laura's house with her extended family and the most amazing buffet.

On our way back to the city on Christmas Night, Laura pulled into a gas station to refuel. I was still in the car when a guy approached Laura and started into a well-rehearsed spiel about homeless veterans. Something struck a chord with me though and I found myself getting out of the car to go talk to him. The thought of how generous family, friends and total strangers had been to me with small contributions, free food and home stays all around the planet that had kept me from being homeless for the last ten months. I opened my wallet and handed him twenty dollars for his chosen charity, the Loaves and Fishes. It's a small fraction of the support I'd received, but I was considering it a first instalment on a debt I'd spend a lifetime repaying.

The day after Christmas, Laura decided Jeremy and I were in desperate need of a mystery tour. We set off on the highway headed east, with Laura keeping our destination secret. She had talked about visiting Lake Tahoe the previous day, but it was an eight hour round trip so it didn't seem likely. As we started to work our way up into the mountains, we realised that maybe she hadn't been joking twenty four hours earlier.

As darkness set in and we gained altitude, the snow got heavier and heavier. The temperature dropped below freezing, and the car was moving around on the snow and ice like a figure skater. As we dropped into the town of South Lake Tahoe, which straddles the California and Nevada state line, Jeremy and I real- ised that without tyre chains we were destined to spend the night in town. The car wouldn't be able to get back over the mountain on the ice without risking an accident.

We went for food and then we had a decision to make. The road was impassable until morning, and the only room available in the entire town was in one of the casinos across the Nevada state line and had a hefty $480 price tag. We didn't have the money between us, Laura was getting tired, and we weren't about to sleep in the car with the temperature a few degrees below freezing.

I made the decision to jump into a poker game in one of the casinos. I'd played a lot of poker and I was all too familiar with pulling all-nighters at a poker table and knew that I'd be warm, with food and drink available all night. Laura and Jeremy set off to find somewhere warm to sleep for free.

Six or seven hours later the game broke up. Not only had I managed to survive the night, I'd made about $400 profit for my evening's work. Jeremy appeared and signalled me to follow him. We made our way out to a Denny's where Laura was waiting. They'd found a place to rest their heads in an unlocked meeting room of one of the casinos across the road. Security had obviously noticed the 'couple' going off the reservation and burst in a little while later expecting, or perhaps hoping, to get an eyeful of something more than a guy and a girl sleeping. Instead, they were banned from that casino and forced to run away when they refused to provide ID. I bought breakfast for the three of us with my winnings, and we watched dawn breaking over the partially-frozen lake before taking our chances with the mountains on our way home.

49
SHINE ON

A sudden succession of shrill rings cut through my dreams. As my eyes opened, I could see the dormitory room in Monterey that I had fallen asleep in, another ring or two rang out before I realised it was my phone. I picked it up and could see I'd a collection of missed calls. Another quick survey of the room, and I realised that I was the only person there. The scenario was eerily familiar. My sister's photo flashed on the screen beside her message: "Can you call me?"

The last time I had kind of expected the news of my grandmother's passing. This time around I had no clue what might have happened, and the time it took for my call to connect seemed like hours. I could tell by her voice that the news wasn't good, I already knew that though.

"Breifne, Aidan died last night," she said.

Her words shook me. Aidan was my eldest cousin, a few weeks short of his 45th birthday. He was a fantastic musician who'd packed in his day job, grabbed his guitar, and spent the best part of 20 years gigging and following his dreams, and plenty of lovely ladies, around Europe. While we were polar opposites in some ways, he was the one person in my family who really understood from the outset exactly what I had planned and why. I couldn't even respond to Kathy on the other end of the call.

I'd promised two of the girls in the hostel that we'd join forces, rent a car, and take a spin to Big Sur later that day. Although my mind wasn't really in it, I didn't want to let the others down, and a few hours later I was driving down the breathtakingly scenic Pacific Coast Highway with two gorgeous girls, and it seemed fitting. It felt like I was about to spend a day perfectly reproduced out of Aidan's very own play book.

My last day in Monterey was the day of Aidan's funeral at home. I'd spoken to his sister Niamh and together we made the decision not to come home for the funeral. I spotted a Chinese cyclist pull into the car park and take a bed in my dorm. I introduced myself to him, and it turned out his name was Ayden. When he invited me to join him for dinner, I couldn't say no. We spent the evening talking about cycling, while in reality my mind was ten thousand kilometres away in Tipperary.

I knew the trip through Big Sur to San Simeon was going to be a struggle. I was facing a 156km ride with some serious climbs along the coast road. This stretch had one of the most spectacular views of the entire trip, and one of the must do stretches of road any touring cyclist should include on their bucket list.

California proved to be a pretty eclectic spot. Some of the highlights included my first visit to In-n-Out Burger with amazing couch surfing hosts Katrina and Erica in San Luis Obispo, being complimented on my spoken English by an Asian receptionist in Santa Maria and trying, unsuccessfully, to convince a twenty-something American girl that Tahoe wasn't an American state.

Jillian's invite to stay in Orange was still good, but she was due to start a new job in San Francisco soon, and we were running out of time. She decided she'd come and collect me in Thousand Oaks, bring me to Orange, and drop me back the next morning.

On my way to Thousand Oaks, I followed the advice of Google Maps and turned off the main road into Wildwood Regional Park. The road was fine until I reached a water treatment works at the end of the road. The road soon became a dirt track, which I guessed would turn back into a road on the other side. By the time I realised I'd guessed wrong, it was too late. I'd already waded through two streams, carrying the bike with my bag holding all my belongings on my back in knee deep, fast moving, ice cold water. It wasn't something I wanted to repeat again.

The route out of the park ended up taking me through an hour-long hike up a dirt track out of the valley, followed by a lengthy trek across the top of the hill, carrying the bike the entire way until I managed to get back on my wheels in the car park beyond. It took half an hour to find a gas station with a suitable area to wash the mud off the bike. Jillian met me at the gas station and soon enough we were back at her house. Her parents, brother and sister were great company and we ended up spending most of the evening talking about her dad's double life as Goofy. In reality, Jillian's dad was a Disneyland engineer, and Jillian's boyfriend Nick had just started the rumour for the fun.

After Gillian dropped me back to Thousand Oaks, I spent the day making my way through Topanga Canyon, meeting the ocean again between Malibu and Santa Monica. The day would see me cycle along Santa Monica, Venice Beach, LAX, and Manhattan Beach before heading inland from Redondo Beach. Fifty kilometres later, I was passing the front door to Disneyland and reached Jillian's family home just after dark. I spent a day at Disneyland courtesy of an invite from Jillian's father. The day at the amusement park was great. I'm not a huge fan of roller coasters, but there was plenty to keep me entertained for the day. I'd expected to only stay a few hours, but I had a lot more fun than even I expected.

50
TAKE IT EASY

Leaving the City of Angels, once again along the Pacific coast towards San Diego, a flat tyre and a complete lack of bike shops along the coast road meant slow going for most of the day. I eventually found an open bike shop and pulled in. One of the three guys at the back of the shop, Brock, walked over to me and asked me how I was. I explained that I was looking for the loan of a pump, as he retrieved a pump he asked me where I'd started my ride.

"Ireland," I said.

"*Cén chaoi a bhfuil tú?*" Brock asked. The Irish phrase meaning "How are you?" was the last thing I'd expected to hear.

"*Ceart go leor agus tú féin,*" I replied, in Irish, translated as "OK and you?"

Brock's hands shot up as he started laughing and admitted that his conversation opener was all he knew in his mother's native tongue. I laughed, and spent a few minutes sharing my story with him and his friends Jim and Bryan.

I continued on south, past Torrey Pines to San Diego and

on to Tijuana to stay with Jono, an old poker buddy from home. After enjoying a few days by the beach in Rosarito, Mexico with Jono and his flatmate Daniel, I was back on the road through the mountains that ran along the US / Mexico border. I would be cycling on the US side of the border and crossing into Mexico to avail of the cheaper accommodation and food on offer each night. The active border patrols both on the road and in the air seemed to make any potential efforts to cross the border illegally seem completely futile.

I crossed into the state of Arizona in the dark, and I found myself reminded of the distances between towns in rural Australia. I got a message on social media from Bryan Staub, one of the trio from the bike shop in San Diego. It turned out that he owned his own cycle clothing company, VR7, and wanted to help me on my journey. Bryan invited me to stay with him, his wife Berry and their young son JD in Phoenix. Bryan mentioned a potential opportunity to speak to a cycling club and told me he had a friend who would service my bike for me in his new shop.

What appeared to be a generous offer turned out to be even better than I'd thought. Bryan gave me a few bits and pieces of VR7 cycling kit, and I got to spend two days at the Phoenix Golf Open where I watched Tiger Woods and met Padraig Harrington before joining a massive Super Bowl party. Then, as Bryan had promised, I was invited to share my story and be the official starter at the Underground Crit. This was a huge honour for me. I got to meet 100 cyclists getting ready for a local weekly criterium race who were fascinated by the idea of cycling around the world.

On one of the best nights of the stay, Bryan took me to meet Jim, another one of the group from the shop in San Diego, at his restaurant, Blue Wasabi. When I told Jim I wasn't a fan of sushi, he started to quiz me about my culinary likes and dislikes, and then gave a series of instructions to the waiter of substitutions for ingredients, spices and sauces and designed five or six plates for the three of us to share. Jim's disgusted face when we attempted to pay for the meal was simply the icing on the cake.

The next few weeks included reliving a classic Eagle's song, taking it easy by standing on a corner in Winslow, Arizona, jumping the Amtrak to Flagstaff to visit Danielle, one of the American girls I'd become friendly with in Goa, and driving to see the utterly amazing Grand Canyon, the beauty of which is not done justice by any photograph I've ever seen.

I met two Irish girls, Rachel and Angela, standing on the rim and we decided to go exploring. They jumped into my rental car and we set off around the edge of the canyon to Moran's Point to find a different, yet equally amazing, view right down the length of the canyon. The girls headed on for Vegas and I was back in the saddle and heading east along Route 66, having my very own American road trip.

51

GET YOUR KICKS
ON ROUTE 66

The cities of Holbrook, Gallup and Grants all came and went as I crossed the Great Divide and I set my sights on Albuquerque, and the two Whitney brothers. John and Fergus had been in primary school with me from the age of four and had both set their eyes on the American dream. As the night was closing in, a bit of light rain and my lights were giving trouble, Fergus came to collect me about twenty kilometres outside the city and I spent the night on his couch. In my original route, I had planned to reach Denver this weekend, but I was a few days short.

I wanted to go to Denver because Martin Silke was the first person to offer me hospitality when I'd announced my plan to cycle around the world. Now residing in Denver, he had set up a series of opportunities for me to talk to members of the Irish community in the Mile High City. In order to make sure that still happened, I hopped onto a Greyhound bus and eight hours later I met Martin at the Denver Bus Station.

On the first day in Denver, Martin introduced me to his boss, Noel Hickey, who owned the Celtic Tavern. Noel was aware of the adventure I was undertaking and when he asked about what my future plans were, I mentioned that I was struggling with my visa expiry date. I told him I would need to leave North America to reset the ninety days I needed to get across the country. I planned to fly to Panama from Dallas for a day or two for that exact purpose.

"Would Costa Rica suffice?" he asked.

I checked the rules and it appeared that Costa Rica would do the trick. He had a friend with a contact in an airline that might be able to sort out cheap tickets from Denver to Costa Rica. He wasn't bluffing. His friend on the other end of the phone line not only had a contact, he had his contact's access codes for the buddy pass ticketing system. I got a return ticket from Denver to San Jose, Costa Rica for just over $100 two days later. Noel then gave me the cash to cover the price of the flights as his token of support. Denver's Irish community was phenomenally supportive, and they pitched together to make a big contribution to the 'Help Get Breifne Home' fund.

It was only when I returned to Denver after my two day sojourn had turned into four that I was informed that the contact in the airline, whose buddy pass I'd been using had actually died two years earlier, but his access had never been revoked. I'd been flying cheap thanks to a dead friend of a friend of a friend of a friend.

Leaving Denver was much tougher than I'd expected it to be. I had missed a sense of community. Solo travel with new locations and new faces around every day was harder than I'd suspected it would be. Seeing a few familiar faces and making friends with plenty of new ones over the days I spent in Denver had been refreshing, but I had to keep going east. A long bus journey back through Colorado Springs, Trinidad and Santa Fe had me back in Albuquerque at nightfall. I woke early the next day, collected my bike from Fergus, and set off to restart the ride.

I didn't get far. It was a particularly cold day when I stopped at a bike shop to pick up some spare tubes. The staff expressed some concern when I suggested I was heading for Santa Rosa or Moriarty along Route 66. Facing a day of climbing into mountains, they told me there had been a snow warning to the east that I was headed right for and the road was unlikely to be passable by bike. I spent some time analysing the weather reports with them in the shop. It didn't look too bad outside the shop, but as I reached the western limits of the city I realised I wasn't going any further that day. The flat plains which lay between the city and the mountains had started to see the wind get a little louder and angrier and the sky above the peaks had turned to a very dark grey, even black in places.

I found the last motel along the strip and got a room to wait it out. It took three days for the ten inches of snow that fell to clear off and allow safe passage into the mountains. I spent most of that with the guys in Two Fools Tavern, the best Irish bar in town and right beside the motel I'd been camped up in.

The first day of March marked the anniversary of the start of the race, and I was finally back on the road, Moriarty, Santa Rosa and Tucumcari, just shy of the Texas border, were to be my stopping points over the coming days. The storm, which had never fully cleared, returned in full force in Tucumcari, New Mexico, a town which was most notable for having nearly half of its buildings burnt to a cinder became the venue for my 34th birthday.

I spent most of the next few days singing the Tony Christie hit 'Is This The Way To Amarillo" to myself while dancing on my pedals along Route 66. Turns out the song that's been number one all over Europe is a virtual unknown in the city itself. My comments about 'Sweet Marie' were totally lost on the locals who kept asking me whether I meant 'Amarillo by Morning'.

Music had begun to play an ever increasing prominence on my ride. I'd been listening to audiobooks and podcasts for most of the journey so far, but certain songs and playlists had started to creep into my listening time on the road. My normal inspirational and motivational playlist had started to be joined by songs which made reference to the region I was cycling through such as Tony Christie's classic, Train's "Save Me San Francisco", 'Santa Cruz' & 'Big Sur' from The Thrills, 'San Diego Song' from The Corona's, "Mexico" by Mundy. I'd already added 'Calling Baton Rouge' by Garth Brooks, 'Johnny B. Goode' with Chuck Berry's opening line of "deep down in Louisiana, close to New Orleans" and 'Sweet Home Alabama" to the playlist for the remainder of my journey across the states.

Authors also featured in a similar way. Steinbeck had been included in Monterey, Michael Connolly's Harry Bosch character joined me in the streets of Los Angeles, and John Grisham would be joining me in Mississippi.

Texas town names like Bowie and Memphis also brought plenty of songs to my mind. Stopping for lunch in the small blink-and-you-miss-it town that shared its name with the Tennessee city which served as Elvis's home, I couldn't resist ordering the catfish special from the menu just to be able to say "There was catfish on the table" as I was "Walking in Memphis".

I stayed with the Hansens in Wichita Falls, touched into Oklahoma simply to tick it off the list, and found myself outside Gordon and Kathy's home in Dallas a few days later. Gordon was an old buddy from my poker playing days, and he brought me to the Sixth Floor Museum at Dealey Plaza, one of the most informative museums I've ever visited. The exhibits explore the events surrounding the death of former US President John F. Kennedy on the street outside the building, from the vantage point of the man who pulled the trigger. The museum even considers and disproves each of the different conspiracy theories which linger to this day.

It was a sobering day, one that will probably stay in my mind forever.

I'd never played baseball before, so Gordon took me to batting practice after our day at the museum. I didn't exactly set the world on fire on my debut, but I had a great time swinging and mostly missing the ball whizzing past my head from the machine at the other end of the cage.

My hopes of getting to visit Austin had to be put on the back burner. The city best known for its music festivals South by Southwest and Austin City Limits, would have to wait for another trip. I'd been offered a place to stay in Houston by Kim Hansen's sister in law, Carolyn, and in the bigger picture the clock was counting down on my flight home to Ireland from Boston. I needed to speed my progress up.

Carolyn insisted that I couldn't miss the Rodeo in Houston if I was passing through. Unfortunately, I was three days away and the final night of the Rodeo was the following day. I explained my predicament that I couldn't skip any portion of the ride at all. Carolyn suggested coming to pick me up and dropping me back to resume my ride later on. I didn't want to put the four hour round trip on her but she wouldn't take no for an answer. I met her in Huntsville the following afternoon and we went straight to the NRG Stadium to experience the rodeo.

There weren't any tickets left for the stadium, just the general admission to the festival around it. Carolyn played the foreigner card to a few of the stewards and they managed to whisk us through the security gate and we made our way to the upper tiers to watch the show. The Rodeo was phenomenal, from cowboys trying to stay on bulls, children trying to wrestle sheep, riders leaping through the air to capture other livestock, and girls on horseback completing speed tests around a set course, I was thoroughly enjoying the night. Then the fun really started.

Within fifteen minutes of the animals and cowboys finishing up, a stage was wheeled into the middle of the 70,000 capacity stadium, and country music superstar Luke Bryan took to the stage. The upbeat tempo of the evening was exactly what I needed. There was one moment though which made me reflect on some of the ways my life had changed irrevocably since I'd started this journey. The lyrics to his song 'Drink a Beer' brought back memories of Aidan, hearing the news of his death over the phone and spending hours staring into the ocean, watching the sunset disappear from the end of a pier in Monterey.

I had made plans to meet up with Stephanie and Dean, two friends from home, the following day. A footballing couple who'd both represented Ireland at various levels, Stephanie had just signed a contract to play professionally in Houston. Carolyn once again offered to be the tour guide, proud to show off the best of what the city had to offer.

We decided on NASA and enjoyed a tour of the control centre made famous by the movie *Apollo 13*. Thankfully we didn't have any problems to report as we enjoyed a sunset meal on the Gulf coast at Galveston before making the return journey to Houston. Carolyn went so far over and above what is expected of any person who offers a weary traveller a place to stay and certainly helped to put the city on my map for a return visit.

52
CALLING
BATON ROUGE

I crossed the state line into Louisiana and decided to stay off the main highway as far as possible. In reality, the only option was the raised highway which ran over a multitude of causeways through the swamps of west Louisiana. I did take the northern route through the state to avoid the worst of the traffic before the roads merged at Baton Rouge and I headed south of Lake Pontchartrain and into New Orleans.

Another former player, Lynn, was now coaching in New Orleans and gave me a place to rest my head for two days in the city. The eclectic mix of cultures in the French Quarter proved fascinating. Bourbon Street was hopping at lunch time with live music everywhere, with entertainers of all kinds visible along the world famous party street. I strolled around, found a bike shop and picked up the necessary spares to get me to Florida.

After taking weeks to get across Texas and days passing across Louisiana, my state count was about to increase rapidly. As I made my way east along the Gulf Coast shoreline, I spent each night in a different state. Bay St Louis, Mississippi was quickly followed by Theodore, Alabama and Pensacola, Florida on consecutive nights. I was glad about the shorter distances across states, but I was taking longer days in the saddle to make sure I could catch my flight to New York.

In Bay St. Louis, I'll never forget arriving in the descending dusk, parking my bike underneath the house and climbing the stairs into the home which rested on stilts about 3 metres above ground level. I spent the evening conversing with my couch surfing hosts while they filled me in on the complete devastation that had hit the area during Hurricane Katrina.

The loss of lives and homes in the area during and immediately after the storm and the resulting 9 metre tidal wave which did most of the damage was still felt a decade later. The neighbours who once occupied the numerous houses which lay between them and the sea some 300 metres away had never returned. Their empty lots were a testament to the devastation of the area, most either couldn't afford to rebuild or didn't want to return. Cycling along the gulf coast, every single house I saw was on stilts. The ones that weren't were in the process of being rebuilt.

Disaster struck, and the whole trip nearly fell apart. Without online access to one of my two bank accounts, I wasn't able to monitor what was in my reserve account. My main account and my PayPal account were totally empty, and I was already over the limit of what I'd allowed myself to ask from my parents. FIT Magazine had changed editors and downsized the publication, with my column being downsized along with it. It was looking pretty bleak.

All I could do was continue to keep going and hope that my campaign funds would support me. I was ten days away from reaching my Aunt's house in West Palm Beach, and with accommodation offers in Florida, New York and Boston, as well as the flight home I'd already bought, I knew I didn't need a whole pile of money to get home to Ireland, where I could work out exactly how I was going to fund the remainder of my journey. With the last two weeks of the trip in the US taken care of and homestays in Ireland already sorted thanks to Cycle Against Suicide, I knew surviving another ten days would buy me an extra four weeks on the road.

My luck ran out in Pensacola. Failing to find a couch surfing host, I went online and booked the cheapest hotel I could find along the highway, thinking everything was signed, sealed and delivered. When I arrived, the receptionist asked for my card and after entering my security code the message 'Transaction Declined' flashed back at me from the machine. I tried my other card just in case some miracle donation had come in that I wasn't aware of.

It hadn't.

I found myself sitting on a bench outside the front door of the hotel. It was almost midnight on a Friday night, past four in the morning at home. No one would even be up to help me, and even if they were, banks would be closed until Monday. It didn't help that the night receptionist wasn't exactly the brightest. I tried to explain my situation to her and ask whether she could accept a credit card from someone else over the phone. She just didn't seem to understand what I was asking her. Her mantra was that all bookings had to come through online, while I tried to explain that because it had just rolled past midnight any online booking would actually be for the following night. After about half an hour she finally appeared to understand what I was trying to say.

I managed to get in touch with my aunt Lily, who was preparing for bed on the other side of the state. After explaining my predicament to her, she spoke to the receptionist and managed to organise me a bed for the night. I had finally managed to get in out of the cold and dark, and into a bed. I showered and sat on the edge of the bed, not knowing what my next move was going to be.

It was nearly a thousand kilometres between me and my aunt's house, and I knew I was in trouble. This was the first time I actually thought that I might not be able to finish the ride. I had one final roll of the dice: I could follow my own advice, be honest about my problems and ask for help. The community that I had built around me had grown to almost ten times the three hundred or so that I had started the campaign with and I could ask them to help me. I knew I was going to write a book about my experience so I had a brainwave. I would ask my supporters to pre-order the book, this book that you're reading right now, pay for it that day and I'd promise to send them a signed copy when I eventually got it finished. The policy of total honesty hadn't done me any harm at all so far and I figured I'd give it a shot again. What did I have to lose?

I recorded a short video where I explained exactly what had happened and asked people to pre-order the book or the DVD, or simply sponsor a room. I set a target of €1,000 which I knew was enough to get me home to Ireland, posted it to Facebook, sent a group email to my list, and went to bed, expecting that my request would fall on deaf ears.

I woke five hours later, picked up my phone, and immediately saw the notifications from the crowdfunding campaign. Family, friends and complete strangers had all offered their support, a small amount per person but with the volume, I was already just over my target of €1,000. I literally jumped out of bed and started hopping with joy around the room. My present solitude had made it hard to remember that people were following my journey. I was excited, but I still had a problem: the crowdfunding money would be in my PayPal account, and it would take two working days before I could turn it to cash. I'd be okay from Tuesday, but this was Saturday morning.

As I pondered how I was going to work my way out of this particular problem, two messages came into my phone. One was from my aunt who told me that she was sending me some money that morning via Western Union. The other was from my former colleague and good friend David Malone back in Dublin. He had seen my video on social media and was apologising for not having sponsored my campaign beforehand and asking the best way he could help. Realising he and I shared the same bank, I asked him to lodge the cash directly into my account, skipping out the triple jump through Indiegogo and PayPal. Within ten minutes, I had myself a decent breakfast and then got back on the road with a content feeling inside that I hadn't felt in years.

I hadn't even considered how I would finance my final leg through Spain, France and the UK to the finish line. It turned out that I was going to get that continued push from the very same community that had just put the wind into my sails. Having reached the target of €1,000 inside the first five hours, the figure was almost €3,000 by the twenty four hour mark and over €4,500 within three days. The budget for the remaining three months of the project was now secure. All I had to do was cycle, eat and sleep over and over again until I reached the finish line and create my own little piece of history.

Back on the road, I rode through Tallahassee, Jacksonville and its beautifully secluded bike paths, then Daytona Beach, which was hosting the national colleges cheerleading competition. I'd be lying through my teeth if I even suggested that I hadn't considered staying in town for an extra night, but I had more important things to be thinking about right now. With all these college students in town for Spring break I was worried I wouldn't find a place to stay. I managed to find a motel in a pretty dodgy part of town. I realised the bar across the road was actually a strip club when darkness fell and the neon lights, which had been almost invisible in the daylight, sprang into action.

I stuck to the A1A highway and the bike paths which ran parallel in parts. I stayed with Harry and Margie in St. Augustine, and Harry rode for most of the next day with me south along the Atlantic Coast. The history lesson Harry gave me as we progressed along the road was priceless. I stayed with Joe and his family in Cocoa Beach, Cape Canaveral where I'd been cycling in sight of the launch areas for so many space missions that I'd grown up watching.

I reached Vero Beach, where I went off route to find a bike supply shop to restock my supply of bicycle tubes. While crossing a train track, I heard and felt a pop, which represented my last tube. I was raging, but luck was with me when looked up to see I was standing outside a bike shop, albeit a shut one. I found a place to stay nearby and settled in for a good night's rest before the final push to West Palm Beach the following day.

I was outside Orchid Island bike shop when they opened. After asking for the tubes, I struck up a conversation with one of the staff. It turned out he was the shop owner, Malcolm, and after hearing about my ride he gave my bike a quick once over and ordered one of the guys to swap out my tyres for brand new ones. They then wouldn't even entertain me paying for any of the items sitting on the counter in front of me. I couldn't believe how lucky I was to receive yet another random act of kindness from someone who hadn't known me ten minutes earlier.

The weather had turned very variable the further south I travelled along the Florida peninsula. Thunderstorms, rain and wind had combined to make my final day much harder than the previous few days along the Atlantic coast. I made contact with my Aunt Lily and Uncle Jimmy, who arranged to meet me at the finish point of my American ride, at West Palm Beach Airport. I was looking forward to a few days rest and recovery after a pretty intense last few weeks.

We timed it perfectly. Their car passed me just a few hundred metres from the terminal building. I had the bike packed into the car in record time and within an hour I was showered and tucked up in bed, content with having completed the largest single leg of the ride.

53
A NEW YORK
STATE OF MIND

I still hadn't worked out exactly how I was going to get to Boston to meet my flight home in two weeks. I'd booked the flight months earlier as proof that I intended to leave the country. My original plan had been to cycle to Boston, but with time running out that hadn't been a realistic option for some time. I had been invited to speak at a number of events by members of the Irish community in New Jersey, New York and Boston, and I wasn't about to miss the opportunity to engage audiences with my core message of positivity.

I had come up with a plan. As the race was all about moving east, any attempt to move north towards New York or Boston would require travel west, and that wouldn't do. The rules also allowed for taking flights when crossing oceans. On a map, New York was east of West Palm Beach and the flight path would involve the aircraft flying out over the western part of the Atlantic Ocean, albeit eventually landing on the same side of the water.

My plan was to fly to New York, get back on the bike and

cycle to Boston to catch my flight home. I suspected it was a bit of a loophole in the rules that I could exploit to get in a few more hundred kilometres in the saddle before returning home for my lap of Ireland with Cycle Against Suicide. The only problem was that I hadn't booked my flight to New York, and everything was looking very expensive at the last minute. Then, I remembered I still had the access codes for the buddy pass account, and discovered a load of much cheaper flights.

I spent a few days in Bergenfield, New Jersey with Gerry & Rosemarie Flood and their family, speaking in a local community church and a local chapter of the Knights of Columbus before having an audience with the Irish consulate on Fifth Avenue in Manhattan and a lot of interviews with the Irish media in New York. From the consulate, Gerry and I took a stroll to Grand Central Station, then rode on the subway to walk down Wall Street to the site where the Twin Towers of the World Trade Centre had stood until September 11th, 2001.

The memorial fountain which stood in the centre of the open space left after the collapse of the towers carried an eerie silence. In the centre of a bustling, noisy city it almost had an air of reflection about it, even all these years later.

No one spoke in more than a whisper. It felt like church as thousands of people moved around the place. It just didn't feel right to even consider taking a picture. In this modern world where everything is documented, very few people if any had cameras in their hands. The serene peace of the shrine was reinforced by the sound of the flowing water around the edge of the monument. People seemed to instinctively follow the unwritten rule.

While I was there, I took the opportunity to catch up with a few old teammates and friends around the city. Rory and his girlfriend Sylwia brought me to see the NY Mets beat the Miami

Marlins in a baseball game, while Aisling, a physiotherapist working with the newest Major League Soccer franchise, New York City FC, hooked me up with tickets to watch them play the Portland Timbers in Yankee Stadium. Despite her side losing by the only goal of the game, she was in good spirits as we got the subway back to the city and I had my first Shake Shack experience.

I stayed one night with Padraic, an old school friend and teammate from my teenage years. His partner Alison and kids Kayla, Ciara and Braden were friendly and full of questions about my cycling and where I'd been to on my journey. Kayla joined Padraic and me as he dropped me back to the airport to restart the journey again. First, I cycled through Newark and Jersey City to reach Liberty Park.

Looking out at Lady Liberty standing proudly in the mouth of the bay, guarding the city from the Atlantic Ocean to the east, I couldn't help but think about how far I'd come already. I hadn't finished the race yet, but the next piece of land in that direction was the Emerald Isle. I'd started the whole journey on the other side of this body of water, and although I had plenty of distance still to cover in the race, I felt like I'd finished. The remainder of the ride would be a lap of honour.

The roads in New Jersey were horrendous, the cities weren't very welcoming, traffic was a nightmare, and the numerous bridges over train tracks and rivers were in places downright scary on two wheels. I continued north until I'd reached Gerry's place in Bergenfield which I would be leaving for good the following morning. It just wouldn't be in quite the way I'd planned.

I'd just got a surprising message from the race organisers. I'd taken so long to finish the race, I honestly thought they had forgotten it was still happening. It turned out someone had complained about my flight from West Palm Beach to New Jersey. I spoke to Dan Wedgewood, director of The Adventurists, the company who had promoted and organised the World Cycle Race. He mentioned that they had scheduled a meeting of the race committee in a few hours' time to discuss the situation in greater detail and needed a response from me.

I explained the rationale of my decision and that I hadn't believed I was breaking any rules, but that I could understand his concerns. I was in limbo. I knew that Lee had been eliminated from the race for a similar reason, after refusing to return to the point of the infringement and restarting his ride.

In anticipation of a similar compromise being offered in this instance, I offered to return to the airport in which I'd landed in New Jersey and continue my journey by scheduled public transport the entire way to Belfast, via New York, Boston and Dublin in order to make my entire journey across the Atlantic stretch a little further than previously planned and including two flights, two train journeys and three buses. All I could do was wait for a return phone call.

I heard back later that day. The committee had decided that although there had clearly been no intention to break rules, my initial interpretation of the rules couldn't be accepted. They had discussed my compromise option and decided that it would suffice to satisfy the rules of the race. Ironically, in the exact same bike race where one competitor had been disqualified for not cycling a stretch of the route, I would have been disqualified had I attempted to cycle a different section of the route. Sometimes, reality can be stranger than fiction.

Twenty four hours after changing in Newark and Manhattan, my bus arrived into Boston. Almost two years earlier, Michelle, another friend from university, had offered me a bed in Boston.

What she couldn't have expected was that I'd arrive in the middle of a perfect storm. The day I arrived, her parents were in town and staying with her and her husband, Mark, for the best part of a month. They were busy babysitting Hannah, Michelle's four week old baby at home in the house she had moved into just a week previously. Did I mention that Hannah had spent almost the first two weeks of her life in Intensive Care and Mark was right in the middle of the busy period of a two-year cycle at work, which meant eighteen hour days six or seven days a week for a month?

Knowing all this was going on, I tried to avoid piling any more stress onto her shoulders, figuring that even Wonder Woman would struggle to keep all those balls in the air. I decided to stay with Alix, who I met while she was travelling along the Great Ocean Road near Melbourne, and who'd also offered a bed for the period I had planned to be in Boston.

I planned to meet Michelle for lunch or something else non-taxing for her, but once my plans changed and I arrived in Massachusetts a few days early she insisted I stay with her.

Even with everything that was going on in her world, Michelle had set up a series of talks and events across the city to help spread the suicide prevention message. Thursday evening saw an invite to the Irish Immigration Centre in Boston. Michelle's friend Danielle was head of the Wellness services in the centre and had invited me to speak. It was great to see so many Irish faces around the room, with some familiar faces from home dotted amongst the crowd. One of the guys I recognised was my near-neighbour Paul McGovern, who invited me to his house on my final morning in the USA. He'd planned a get together of some other people originally from around Leitrim but now living in Boston for a send-off breakfast. I was honoured to be invited and immediately agreed.

Michelle and her family had been at the talk, but in order to give her a little relief I'd agreed to stay with Alix for the next two or three nights until my flight home on Sunday evening. I'd be meeting Michelle again at the soccer game on Saturday evening. Months earlier, Michelle had engineered an invite from the local Major League Soccer team, the New England Revolution, for me to be the "Hero of the Game" at their clash that weekend.

In addition to the invitation to attend the game, this honour involved my being brought out onto the pitch just before kickoff, and my face beamed onto the jumbotron screen behind one of the goals while the announcer told the crowd about the challenge that I was in the process of undertaking and my motivation for taking it on. Hearing the mantra "It's OK not to be OK" broadcast to 23,000 people was one of the highlights of the trip, and the warm reception from the stadium and local fans was matched by the social media love that came from the great people of New England.

The following morning I was sitting at the breakfast table with a group of Leitrim people eating full Irish fried breakfasts as the conversation flowed easily. It was an eye opener watching all these people who had moved to Boston to make a life for themselves that they just weren't able to find at home. None of them showed any real desire to move home, and seemed to be really enjoying life with their families on the other side of the Atlantic.

I'd also managed to meet Emlyn Mulligan when in Boston. He had been the captain of the Leitrim football team for a few years and had decided to take a year out and travel, ending up in Boston, where he'd moved with his partner Elaine. They were working here for the summer and he was playing a bit of football. We'd been in touch, and Alix took me to meet him and Elaine for coffee and we sat for an hour or two just chatting about our travels and the travails of being the underdog in a sporting context.

It was finally time to return to Europe. I met Michelle and collected my bike from her, and just like that I was on my way home. Fourteen months after leaving Ireland, I was finally going to be back on Irish soil.

IRELAND

27th April - 10th May, 2015

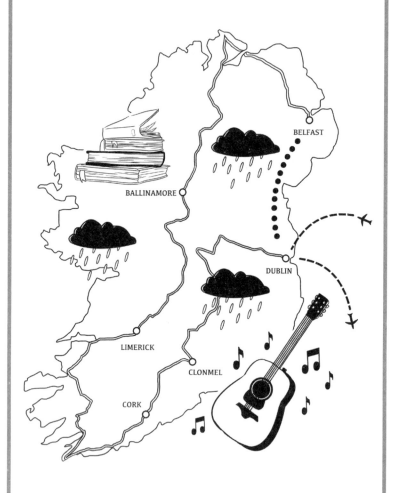

Distance: 1,391km

Elevation: 9,505 metres

54
HOMEWARD
BOUND

Dublin's passport control seemed to take forever, and then having to wait until everyone had left the baggage reclaim area before collecting my bike didn't help. Of course, when things start to roll against you everything joins in, and Customs wanted a look inside the box to ensure I wasn't smuggling anything into the country. When I finally emerged through the sliding doors I was faced with my entire family, who'd travelled up from Leitrim at an unearthly time of the morning to meet me.

My uncle Dermod, my neighbours Shauna and Aimee, and Colm from Cycle Against Suicide were there too. I'd not really expected to see them all there, and was a little bit taken aback by the whole emotion of the morning.

After grabbing a quick bite to eat I had to run for a bus, the final leg of my extended transit from the United States to the start line of the route earmarked for Cycle Against Suicide in Belfast.

Cycle Against Suicide is a two-week cycle around the entire island of Ireland, stopping in schools twice daily sharing a positive mental health and suicide prevention message. A wide range of speakers offer their personal experiences to the assembled audiences which normally includes school children, teachers and members of the community.

I joined some old friends and plenty of new faces at the fire station in the centre of the city. With time ticking down, I rebuilt my bike out of the box and managed to get myself sorted just in time as people started to congregate for the safety briefing for the day's ride to Coleraine on the northern tip of the island.

The cold and wet weather was a complete shock to my system, which had been spoiled by the temperate climate of Florida for my last cycling days a week or two previously. On the second morning, my host Donal presented me with shoe covers and gloves. This was essential kit that I hadn't needed in over a year since leaving Europe the first time around.

I'd been looking forward to the event since I'd signed up months beforehand. I'd been invited along to share my story in the schools along the way and I was looking forward to contributing to the discussion around mental health promotion.

As a rule, I'd been hanging out at the back of the group, allowing a nice divide between me and the next person around me in order to avoid infringing the drafting rules of the World Cycle Race. With a twenty kilometre an hour speed limit on the entire group, drafting wouldn't even have helped.

With a few eagle-eyed followers around, including one or two people on social media who would have taken great satisfaction on my being eliminated at this late stage, I chose to withdraw a little from the group to avoid any random picture showing up somewhere that would cast aspersions on my ride or require any explanation at all.

As a football coach, I've always preached to my players about not creating an opportunity for the referee to make a biased decision. I wasn't going to give anyone the opportunity to create any potential question marks about my adherence to the rules.

With photographers and video cameras floating everywhere I spent a lot of my focus on ensuring I was never gaining any advantage from drafting off other cyclists or vehicles.

The first significant input I had into the proceedings came on day four, after I was asked by Kevin Finn, one of the charity directors, to lead the entire group into our lunch stop in Ballinamore, County Leitrim.

It was a huge honour to be leading a few hundred cyclists into my home county, and my mother's home town. To my knowledge, it was the first time such an honour had been given to anyone by the organisation.

In Ballinamore, I was introduced briefly and answered a few questions about the countries I'd cycled through.

A week later, in Cork, I was delighted to be asked to speak again. I got a very early morning text from the master of ceremonies, asking me to speak.

"Morning Breifne."

"Morning."

"Want to say a few words this morning at the school? You haven't spoken for a while."

"I'd love to. I'll be there shortly just in traffic at the moment. How long do you want me to speak for?"

I didn't get a reply.

I went along to the talk that morning, and mixed with the other speakers, which included some personal friends. I stood at the side of the sports hall as each of the other speakers was called, handed the microphone, and given the floor to share their story and their learnings from their experiences. Every one of the speakers was invited, except for me. I was beginning to realise that something was off.

When I got off the bike at lunch time I noticed that while I'd been cycling I'd received a reply to my previous message.

"Ran out of time today, sorry. I really appreciate your flexibility."

At the end of the break stop I was approached asking if I'd received the message, I nodded and explained how I felt very excluded after having been invited to participate and being told I would be part of the proceedings.

It felt like I had been dismissed.

I had a feeling I would no longer be involved in the official portion of any of the presentations. I decided to fade back into the group and focus on just cycling the distance. I was looking forward to sharing the last few days in Ireland with the amazing people I'd met over these two weeks, and I'd be back on my own in a few days in Northern Spain and away from the politics and personalities soon enough.

The weather was horrific. In Clonmel, as we were leaving a girls' secondary school, a number of the students joined us. Most of the girls, as well as a smaller portion of the novice older cyclists in the group, were ill-equipped and not dressed appropriately for the extreme weather conditions, just normal shorts and t-shirts. The rain had soaked through to the skin before they'd even reached the edge of the town. Foil blankets and towels were already being used by nearly half the group at the first small break half an hour into the day. At the half-way point, in Thurles, nearly everyone was wearing a foil wrapper and trying to get and stay warm. The number of teenagers who were shivering with blue lips and ghostly white faces was scary. The decision was made to cancel the second half of the day.

This left me with a bit of a dilemma. While everyone else was waiting on a bus to Portlaoise, I knew I couldn't ride it under the rules of the World Cycle Race. My two choices were either to brave the elements and make it to Portlaoise this evening or to stay in Thurles, hope for better weather tomorrow, start early, and catch the crew before they made it to the next stop Mullingar the following day.

I sought out one of the event marshals or the race director to explain my predicament, and as I was explaining my situation to him, I heard the words 'cycled around the world' coming from the speakers, followed by my name. Rob Carley was calling me to the stage. I made my way up to the top of the room, where Rob invited me to share my story with the few hundred people in the room. For the next five or six minutes I shared my experience of overcoming suicidal thoughts and turning my life around by setting positive goals, and how that brought me to cycle around the world and on the brink of winning the World Cycle Race.

I was blown away by the enormous round of applause I got from the students, their teachers and the cyclists who were gathered around the sides of the hall. All the self-doubt and questioning of whether I'd really achieved anything over the previous fourteen months on the bike evaporated.

After the talk finished I told Christy, one of the race marshals, that I was heading off and not waiting on the buses. One of the guys I'd been chatting to during the cycle heard me and offered to come with me. I was most appreciative of the company and we set off. We stopped after an hour for a little break and to warm up a little. Still wet and cold, having the extra layers around the body certainly helped. Donal's gift of the shoes and gloves all the way back in Coleraine certainly came in handy in these wintery conditions.

As we prepared to get back on the road we spotted a blur of orange flashing past and they came to a stop. Eight other cyclists led by Christy had set out after us to catch us. They had been working together as a rolling group each taking turns at the front and then a prolonged turn of tucking in behind the others to shelter from the elements.

I explained the rules of my scenario to the group, and nominated myself to take the brunt of the weather, as the rules forbid any form of drafting. I imagine that while the weather was unpleasant for all of us, the others surely got some benefit in tucking in behind my ample posterior to protect themselves from the elements.

Pulling into Portlaoise soaked to the core, we were less than a mile from the end when a tyre punctured. The entire group stopped and adopted a 'One for All, All for One' approach. It took ten or fifteen minutes to fix the flat in that awful weather, but the ten of us all crossed the finish line together.

The last two days were a little bit special for me. I was joined by one of my couch surfing hosts, Ellen, whose family I'd stayed with in Eden, New South Wales. She wasn't an accomplished cyclist, but she really got into the spirit of the event and joined us on the mornings of both of the final two days of the ride.

The excitement on the last day was beginning to filter through the crowd, which had grown considerably as the weekend arrived. Leaving Mullingar, the peloton stretched out for almost a mile and the group slowly made its way through the satellite towns approaching Dublin. Kinnegad, Enfield, Leixlip before the roads were closed off along our main approach to the city.

The rolling road closures continued as the entire north quay was closed to allow the group through uninterrupted, heading for Merrion Square and towards the finish line in RTE's campus at Montrose. Everyone stayed around and music was blaring, food and drink were endless and the hugs seemed to go on forever as people eventually started to fade into the distance.

My parents and my uncle Dermod were at the finish line. I spotted them in the crowd as I approached. Since I hadn't expected them, it was great to see their familiar faces in the hundreds of people that were gathered. They drove back to the family apartment just around the corner and I made the short cycle back after having put most of my belongings in the boot of their car.

Ellen was staying with me for a few days, and now it was my turn to repay the tour guide favour. There's nothing quite like being a tour guide in your own country. I'm extremely proud of the small island I hail from, particularly my own home county of Leitrim and the northwest area in general.

Over the few days, I brought Ellen to visit the megalithic stone tomb at Newgrange, the grave of W.B. Yeats in Drumcliffe churchyard under Ben Bulben's watchful eye, and the serenely beautiful Glencar Waterfall in north Leitrim.

I'd had so much hospitality shown to me not just from Ellen's family but from everyone from old friends to complete strangers driving hundreds of miles to accommodate me. Across each country I'd cycled through, all sorts of time, finance and accommodation options were offered to me to make my life easier and cheaper. It will probably take me my entire life to pay back my debt to the couch surfing community, not necessarily to the same people who helped me but other members of the collective who might pass onto my radar over the years.

My flight to Santander, Spain was in the early afternoon of Wednesday. My marathon friend Liam joined me in the airport for a light lunch and quick catch up.

After making my way through security I was once again on my own, facing into a new country, a different language and a brand new culture on the Iberian peninsula.

Two of the deepest words in the English language when used together are 'The Last'. Putting those words before virtually any word conveys significant meaning. This entire adventure had been about a huge journey, but nearly all epic adventures in this century are measured in flying time. This would be 'The Last Flight' of my route.

It was my first 'Last' of the journey and it began to sink in that my entire adventure was nearing its close. I didn't have long to dwell on the significance of this leg of the trip until my plane touched down and I was alone, in northern Spain, on a bike, and with no place sorted to stay that evening.

The usual, really.

WESTERN EUROPE

15th May - 4th July, 2015

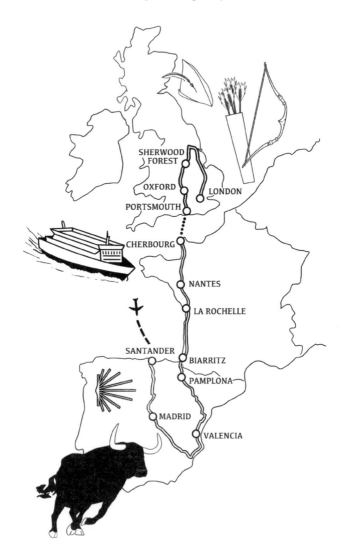

SHERWOOD FOREST

OXFORD

LONDON

PORTSMOUTH

CHERBOURG

NANTES

LA ROCHELLE

SANTANDER

BIARRITZ

PAMPLONA

MADRID

VALENCIA

Distance: 3,910km

Elevation: 27,324 metres

55
HOLIDAY
IN SPAIN

As I had done so often before on arriving in a new country, I'd found a nice spot to rest my head in Santander. I gave myself a day to adjust to the hotter climate, plan my route, and restock my supplies. On the Cycle Against Suicide, I had the support of hundreds of other cyclists, in addition to support buses and vans for the last two weeks.

Cycling in a group had been a big help but it hadn't been without its frustrations. At times, we would stop for lengthy group breaks when I was just hitting my groove. At other times, we were taking on mountain passes when my legs just weren't feeling it that day. Sticking to a schedule had its own challenges.

Now, I was in the north of Spain, preparing for a few lengthy days of climbing into the Galicia Mountains between the coast and the city of Burgos. I woke up early to hit the slopes, and I was disgusted with myself for only then discovering that the brakes on the bike were completely shot.

I eventually found a bike shop where they could be repaired, and ate a late breakfast while the mechanics worked on the problem. I was on the road two hours later than I'd initially planned. It had taken a while to get out of the city of Santander. I was on my own again by the time I found the road I was due to take towards the south.

I was also struggling with my Spanish. My pigeon French and German had been enough to get me through most of Europe a year earlier, but English wasn't very common in this part of Spain, and my Spanish was awful.

At one restaurant I'd stopped by for lunch, the waitress actually brought me into the kitchen and pointed at different ingredients with a thumbs up and a thumbs down used to indicate whether to include it in my meal or not.

It was embarrassing. For the first time in a while, I needed to put some work into my language skills.

I had picked a town on the map that I had planned on staying in, Pte de El Escuda. I had made good time, and over the course of the day, the road had risen gradually from sea level in Santander to about 350 metres above the sea fifty kilometres further up the road.

This was easier than I had anticipated. After lunch I spotted a signpost for Pte de El Escuda, and it was only seven kilometres away.

"This is easy," I thought to myself. "I'll be there in half an hour at this rate."

I hadn't factored in the sudden increase in the gradient. An hour after lunch, I wasn't anywhere near my target. Worse yet, the sheets of rain and the cold, cutting wind had combined to make the whole day miserable, the road ahead just disappeared into the clouds in the distance.

As I progressed up the mountains, the clouds stayed at the

same elevation, and I cycled right into the cloud cover. Visibility was down to a few metres in both directions, and the entire atmosphere became very wet.

It was raining, but I was actually cycling through the clouds. It was a surreal experience - a feeling like being in a swimming pool full of deep, wet fog instead of water.

On the road markers, the numbers to the town continued to drop until eventually I reached it. This was a problem, largely because there wasn't a town. I had made a mistake, 'Pte de' was short for 'Puerto de' which translates to English as 'Gate' or 'Port'. It was a gate through and over the mountain. There was nothing here except a pillar on each side of the road and a sign marking the spot, informing me that I was more than a kilometre above sea level.

I started to panic. There wasn't a town marked on the map for some distance. I was freezing cold, I was wet, and my extremities were beginning to tingle with pins and needles. There was maybe an hour of daylight left, and I had no hope of making it to the next town on the map. Looking into the valley the road dropped into, there was a climb of about 300 metres on the other side, which I seriously doubted I could have managed, I was so tired.

I started freewheeling down into the valley. From the top point, visibility may well have been zero. As I dropped below the cloud cover, I finally got the chance to survey the landscape. There was an enormous lake off to the right hand side of the road, with the ruins of an old castle to the left.

There was a small settlement in the valley ahead, but it hadn't been on the map. In my current state, my eyes were drawn to the road rising on the other side until it disappeared into the clouds. I didn't fancy my chances.

* * *

The village turned out to have a small pub and restaurant. I tried to explain I was looking for somewhere to stay.

"Yes, we have rooms upstairs," said Pilar, the girl behind the counter, in almost perfect English

I felt like I was in heaven. My bike was put into the secure lock up beside the dirt bikes and the motor boats. It looked like people around here really knew how to have some adventure fun. I showered, ate and fell asleep all in about an hour. Then, I woke up in another world.

By morning, the skies were blue and the temperature had moved a full twenty degrees up the scale. My water problem had gone from being surrounded by it to making sure I had enough of it. There weren't many options for refuelling before I'd get to the city of Burgos.

Thankfully, the early morning legs and the good weather meant I made easy work of the first climb up to the second pass of the route. The view from the top was amazing, and the mountains on the other side of the valley would mean I had my day's work cut out for me. I crossed the valley and at the base of the mountain I found a little restaurant for lunch.

The next twelve kilometres took me nearly an hour. The climb back up to over one thousand metres above sea level was draining, but the weather made it a lot more pleasant than the experience had been the previous day.

I had some fun and games as I approached Burgos. The city is a popular stopping point along the Camino de Santiago, and I suspected that accommodations would be expensive. My phone wasn't able to pick up a data signal so I went looking for a place to stay the old-fashioned way. I spotted a hotel and made my way inside.

The two girls behind reception at the hotel made me suspicious I had walked into Fawlty Towers. The first girl, let's call her Manuela, after the famous Spanish waiter from Fawlty Towers, wasn't sure whether or not they had a vacancy. The second girl, who we'll call Manuel-b, also didn't have any clue. Eventually Manuela decided they had a room, but that it was going to set me back €70 for the night. Knowing that normal rates along the Camino can be less than €10 in places, I was sure there must be a cheaper option. Manuel-b told me that the city was entirely full, and that this hotel had the only vacancy in town.

I knew I could do better. I asked the girls for the password for the hotel's Wi-Fi, which Manuel-b refused to give up until I'd rented a room. Meanwhile, Manuel-a had found a webpage listing local accommodations, all at much lower rates. The damage had been done, but Manuel-a tried, unsuccessfully, to convince me that I wouldn't want to stay in any of those places.

I eventually wound up at the first hotel on the list, just four blocks away, and parted with twenty five euro for a lovely room, then took my time enjoying the equally-affordable restaurant next door.

When I left the city, I couldn't help but notice the number of people travelling on bikes seemed rather large for a Sunday. It turns out a local bicycle festival had organised rides for all ages in every town and city along my route. I spent most of the morning weaving in and out of groups of cyclists along the fantastic bike paths south of Burgos. It was great to see people of all ages, from kids with stabilisers to grandparents cycling along together. I waved at everyone who passed me in the opposite direction with a large smile on my face for most of the day. There's something quite beautiful about seeing a young child on their first ride or an elderly couple out for a casual spin together.

It helped that the weather was amazing, with blue skies above and the vineyards of northern Spain nestled on either side of the small single lane roads running parallel to the main highways, I found myself daydreaming my way through the hilly terrain. It was as if I was cycling through a landscape painting of greens and blues.

When I arrived in Aranda, the owner of the hostel I had booked was nowhere to be found. When I called the number on the listing, he screamed down the phone at me in speedy Spanish. I had no idea what he was saying. I eventually wandered back to a small cafe at the end of the street to find a friendly local. I tried explaining myself, and eventually one man realised what I was looking for. He rang another hostel.

I was made to feel like I was inconveniencing the manager of the second hostel. I really haven't had a good experience of Spanish hospitality – it just felt grumpy. People spoke little or no English, and didn't seem prepared to meet me half way when I made an, admittedly poor, attempt at their language. I hadn't experienced such bad manners in the places one expects it, like India, Malaysia, Thailand, or Turkey. Spain was falling behind in my opinion.

Finding food on a Sunday evening proved even harder. I eventually found a bar where Barcelona was playing on the television, but there was no food, so my dinner was a tiny sandwich and a glass of coke. I was going to enjoy breakfast.

I spent most of the next day climbing a winding road up to over 1,500m as I crossed into the province of Madrid at Alto del Leon. I was entirely wrecked, but the view of the Spanish capital city sprawling out into the distance below was phenomenal. I enjoyed the fifteen kilometre descent into the small village of Alpedrete, where I met up with Wendy, a friend from Dublin who was studying there hidden away in the mountains on the northern outskirts of Madrid.

I made the decision to avoid the main city of Madrid by skirting to the ring roads on the west of the city. That was when disaster struck. My chain had been slipping for a few days, and I'd spent more than enough time getting it back on the gears. Now, the front chain ring decided to join the party. The chain was slipping regularly, sometimes just coming off completely. I eventually found a bike shop, and had to replace the chain and the rear cassette.

These repairs fixed most of the problems, but I had to reach the Mediterranean coast, 500km away, inside the next four days, I wasn't in a position to wait twenty four hours for a non-essential part, which left me with a slightly limited range on the bike. As long as I didn't use the big ring at the front, I would have no problems. The harder gears were now off limits, unless I was willing to risk the chain falling off. Again.

The reason behind my deadline to get to Guardamar was pretty straightforward. I'd been invited by a friend, AJ Leon, to speak at his conference, Misfit Con, back in the US.

I'd first met AJ a few months before I started the race, and fast forward eighteen months and he sent me a message inviting me to tell my story in Fargo at Misfit Con.

A few weeks earlier, when I was in his home town of New York, AJ and I had a call on Skype while he was visiting Dublin, where I had been living for fifteen years. We joked about the irony of us talking to each other from each other's hometowns on opposite sides of the globe.

On the call, I explained to AJ that all my resources were occupied with the race, and that I couldn't justify spending what at this point was my supporters' hard-earned cash, regardless of how good an opportunity it might be to share my message with an entirely new audience.

"What if cost wasn't an issue?" AJ asked, setting the tone.

"I'd be there with bells on!" I replied.

Ten minutes later, I had an airline ticket in my email and a hotel room in Fargo, North Dakota.

I was hoping to reach Guardamar Del Segura. My parents have a small holiday home near the beach there, and my sister Kathy and her family were going to be in town when I got back from the States.

I was planning on leaving the bike and my equipment there, fly to Fargo for the conference, and return to pick up the bike before my final stretch through Spain, over the Pyrenees and the west coast of France, to the finish line in London, and then, finally, home.

Four days later I was sitting in the Shamrock Bar in Guardamar, facing into a massive serving of gammon steaks put on by Walter and Jacqui, who had been in touch throughout my journey.

They were preparing to host a party for me once I'd returned from Misfit Con. I spent the day off emptying, tidying and repacking each of my bags. I needed a lot less stuff for the conference than I needed on the bike.

I hopped on the bus to the airport, and five hours later made it to the check in desk. I took no time clearing security and as I prepared to order breakfast I reached for my wallet only to discover I didn't have it.

I searched my pockets and bag, and there wasn't a sign of it anywhere. I had used it to pay for my bus ticket the previous evening, and I had a vision of slipping it into the small pocket on the back of the seat in front of me.

No matter. I had nothing on me. No money, no cards, and no way to fix it. Due to the clean-up the previous day, all of my emergency cards and money I'd secreted in separate places wasn't where I'd left it.

For the first time in over a year, I put my cards and cash together, and 12 hours later both were missing. It was just me, my boarding passes and my passport.

I found a kiosk in the airport that offered a half hour's free internet, and got messages to AJ and Melissa. I cancelled my cards and ordered new ones, which my sister would be able to bring to me. I offered to send AJ money via PayPal in exchange for the equivalent when I landed, and the disaster was averted. I was able to breathe a little sigh of relief.

I now just had to survive three flights and two stop-overs in New York and Chicago over 24 hours without any money. My stomach was already rumbling, and I was praying that the airplane food was going to be both tasty and plentiful.

I came home from Misfit Con with a whole new lease on life. Between the physical rest and meeting some amazing people who had done amazing things, from building companies and employing tens of thousands of people, to setting up worldwide socially beneficial movements, art, education & social projects in some of the poorest and disadvantaged parts of the world, I was surrounded by inspiration.

My sister and her boys picked me up at the bus station and we had a great day or two hanging out at the beach. I joined Kathy and her family for a meal the next afternoon. We were just around the corner from the pub when a conversation came up about the uses of waterproof tea-bags, inflatable dart boards, striped paint and the like.

I decided to have a bit of fun and I asked my fourteen year-old nephew, Matthew, to run across to the Shamrock and ask for a "Long Stand."

Ten minutes later, he hadn't returned. Cathal, Kathy's partner followed him over to find him standing beside the door.

Seemingly the Irish owner, Jacqui, had realised the prank and replied to his request with, "Absolutely, I'll get it for you in a moment, I'm just dealing with this customer."

After she'd passed him repeatedly, ignoring him each time, he had repeated his request.

"I'll be right with you, it's out in the store room," was her reply.

"Does a Long Stand mean standing here like an idiot for a long time?" Matthew asked Cathal.

Cathal's reaction told him everything he needed to know. He did see the funny side of it eventually, though.

The next morning, I got a send-off from outside the pub as members of the local community came to say goodbye and Dylan, Eoin and Ken even cycled a bit of the way with me.

I made my way up along the Mediterranean coast through Alicante, Benidorm and Valencia before staying with Laura, an old college friend, now teaching in Castellon de la Plana. She invited me to speak to her school assembly the next morning and it was a very enjoyable experience. Some of the kids were as young as five or six years of age.

After showing them a video of my travels, they were gobsmacked about the whole journey, but their questions were very insightful. Most were about the places I'd seen, the animals I met along the way, how much water I drank and how I got my bike across the seas and oceans.

Accommodation proved to be the hardest thing to find for the remainder of my time in Spain. I'd accidentally ended up on the Camino de Santiago from Castellon. The towns were a little bit further apart the more I moved inland from the Mediterranean. I ventured back into the hills through Zaragoza and on to Pamplona before I had to climb the Pyrenees.

Although the Pyrenees were only half the height I'd reached on the approach to Madrid, they were difficult work. The rain and the colder temperatures were proving difficult.

As I left Pamplona, slightly disappointed I hadn't spotted any bulls roaming the streets, I found myself at the mouth of a tunnel. A quick Google search told me I was facing a ten kilometre detour to avoid going through the tunnel, but it didn't appear that long, and I saw daylight clearly visible at the other end, about half a kilometre through the mountain. Better yet, the hard shoulder alongside the road appeared nice and wide. I decided to take my chances with the darkness, certain I wasn't supposed to be there, but prepared to plead ignorance of the rules of the road.

In hindsight, that was not the brightest move. It was as if every truck in town had been notified of my presence in the tunnel, and they were playing a game to see how close they could get to the edge of the road and then gain bonus points for any speed wobbles they might cause me to take.

I spent the rest of the day climbing once again into rain-soaked mountains. The switchback climbs left me catching my breath each time I made a turn, as the steep falls just the other side of the small barrier were terrifying. Eventually I needed to take refuge under the shade of a tree as the sheets of rain started to intensify.

Late in the evening, I found myself at the mouth of yet another tunnel. This time, no daylight was visible from the other end. The signage told me I faced two and a half kilometre ride through the mountain. I wasn't feeling so confident this time around.

I elected to roll a little back down the mountain and take the old road that had been indicated on the road signage, this resulted in me facing a higher climb on an unused road across the top of the mountains.

Looking down at the main road in the valley beneath me, I realised just how much higher the road had taken me. The descent on the other side of the mountain was really fun before I rejoined the main road at the bottom of the range.

I found a hostel in the town of Oronoz-Mugaire and tucked myself in for a well-earned rest for the night. Tomorrow would see me cross into France for my last land border crossing of the trip. This would be another "last" that would bring me another step closer to the finish line.

56
THE FRENCH CONNECTION

Even though I overslept, it was mostly downhill for the day's ride to the French border and the city of Biarritz, where I intended to stay the night. As was my normal habit most mornings, I planned out my route as I grabbed breakfast. As I prepared to go, the front door opened up and another cyclist came in. We eyed each other somewhat suspiciously before I asked Martin where he was headed.

"Sweden!" Martin replied.

Martin had left Tarifa, the southernmost point of both Spain and mainland Europe, and had set his sights on reaching the very north of the continent: his home country of Sweden. We compared routes and discovered we were planning on riding in the same direction for the next few days. When he ordered his lunch I knew we were going to hit it off.

"Uno bocadillo, jabon y queso, por favor," Martin ordered - the exact same order that I'd been leading with for the previous two weeks.

We ended up riding together to the French border by following the excellent bike paths that ran parallel to the motorway until we faced a decision. We'd followed the path along the river bank until we came to a fork in the road.

The left-hand fork was into the mouth of a pitch-black tunnel, while the right hand option took us up the hill and closer to the river. We tried the hill for a while until the slope got too steep, and then the path ran out. We cut our losses and turned around.

I followed Martin in walking through the tunnel, my headlight battery was dead and with no torch I had to follow Martin's route through the darkness. About half a kilometre through the tunnel, the end came into sight, but we'd barely gotten out when we could see there was another tunnel just ahead of us.

Martin spotted a light switch on the wall and we joked about how handy it would be. I jokingly flicked it and, lo and behold, the darkness turned bright in front of our eyes! We cycled through the series of tunnels, helped by the lights which guided us, until we reached the town of Irun and crossed the border into France.

We stayed in Biarritz and made good progress together over the next few days. Since we had partnered up, we also saved on accommodation costs. Travelling solo can be very expensive, but it rarely costs extra to have a second body in the room. Pairing up meant we both halved the cost, allowing us to get slightly nicer digs and save money.

Just as we approached the city of Arcachon we had started to see signs for the tallest sand dunes in Europe. Our view of the Atlantic had been blocked for most of the day by a combination of the forest and high dunes. We decided to take a few minutes to stop and see what all the fuss was about. Turns out what I had been considering high sand dunes weren't even in the same league as Dune du Pilat.

The sand mountain rose into the sky, and more than two

hundred concrete steps brought us from the base of the sand to almost near the top. From that vantage point we could see over the ocean to the other side of the bay on one side, and an extensive forest stretched out inland and south along the coast as far as the eye could see behind us. We ran down the entire 100m of the sand dunes, barely hitting the ground along the way.

The next morning we caught the ferry across the bay and continued up the west coast. The bike paths were getting better, surrounded by forests for dozens of kilometres, passing in and out of small towns until we reached Montalivet. We were aiming to get the first ferry across the estuary to Royan where we would go our separate ways: I was going north to Cherbourg, Martin was going to Paris and across the continent.

A wrong turn left us under pressure to make the ferry before a two-hour wait would spoil our ambitious plans for the afternoon's progress. Luckily, a sprint for the last hour saw us make the ferry with about six minutes to spare. Martin went his own way, and I set my target on La Rochelle before arriving at Nantes to stay with Lisa, a friend from school.

By this point, my bike was once again in need of some serious repairs. A few spokes had come loose, and I needed a new bag for the space between my crossbar and the steering wheel.

Over a few days in Nantes waiting to get the bike fixed, I caught up on my messages, including a Skype call with Suzie Pike, a Scottish girl who was asking me for advice about planning a cycle across Australia.

Two days later, I became very excited. When I came over a small rise in the road, the Atlantic coast came into view ahead of me, as did Mont St Michel, one of the most iconic French tourist attractions.

I took a detour to take advantage of the opportunity to cycle up the causeway to the front gates of the island settlement before continuing along my planned route. The detour kept me from making the Thursday ferry at the time I'd planned to catch it.

I arrived in Cherbourg a few hours after it had departed, then settled for the next ferry the following day, which would be my last non-cycling portion of the ride.

57

THE FINISH LINE

After a ferry ride full of great laughs, I had returned to England and settled into Noble's house that evening just north of Southampton.

London, as the crow flies, was barely a day's ride to the east, but the race required me to complete 18,000 miles before crossing the line. I had missed out on the portion between New York and Boston that I hadn't cycled. I had to find a route to make up those four hundred or so kilometers, plus a few extra just to be safely over the distance required by the race. I decided I would head due north until I'd completed half of the extra distance, then turn around and head straight back to the capital.

Oxford and Stratford-upon-Avon were behind me by the time I bumped into Adam Holder on the road outside Birmingham. He'd been following my progress since early in the trip, and insisted on looking after me when I arrived in his neck of the woods.

A family visit had kept him from offering me a bed, so he sorted me a room in a nearby hotel, which was well over and above what I'd expected. Although we'd never met in person before that day, it felt like chatting to an old friend.

Kevin Cunniffe, who'd been at the start of the race, offered me a place to stay in Derby, then rode out to guide me to his home. The next day he led me out to the north towards Doncaster, past Nottingham and Sherwood Forest. From there, I finally reached Selby where Adam Browne, an old college friend and former flat-mate, had arranged to meet me.

Adam had recently moved to the UK and was waiting to start a job in London, so he offered to join me for the last three days. The following day, with Adam carrying most of my bulky gear and baggage, I was suddenly feeling tonnes lighter than I had been feeling on the bike for a very long time.

I made great progress to the Humber Bridge, then turned to cross it along the bike path on the east side of the bridge.

Once again, I'd had another pretty big "last." It was my last major turn this side of London. I was now for the first time making progress in a straight line, towards the finish line.

I was beginning to enjoy the extra speed and eventually found myself taking my eye off the ball a little bit. I can't remember exactly what happened, but as I moved to avoid a pothole on a back road I got a little bit too cocky and found myself stumbling and falling off the bike, landing ungracefully in a pile of body and bike.

Thankfully, my pride took more of a hammering than my body did, although I picked up a large bruise all across my chest.

Ten kilometres later, having picked myself up, dusted myself down, and continued cycling, disaster struck again. I had planned another one hundred kilometres for the evening, but all of a sudden I heard a crack, and something fell off the bike. I pulled up just in time. The hanger which holds the rear derailleur had snapped.

Had I continued even another half pedal, I'd have pulled the mechanism through the entire back wheel. This wasn't a problem I would be fixing on the side of the road.

I rang Adam with my location and he set out to find me. In the meantime, I tried finding shops within driving distance that might be able to fix the problem immediately. It was a Wednesday evening around half three in the afternoon. The first five shops I called either didn't have the right replacement parts or their mechanic was off for the evening.

I had told everyone I was going to be in London on Saturday afternoon. Now, it looked like I'd be disappointing them.

Adam arrived, having discovered that our best bet was to bring my bike to a shop in Lincoln, almost eighty kilometres away, at ten in the morning. We decided to go immediately, stay overnight, and be ready to go first thing in the morning. We settled on the idea, but something didn't quite sit right with me. I was concerned that I would lose half of the day just watching the mechanic fix the damage.

Halfords aren't usually regarded as a good option for high-end bikes, but upon seeing that they were open late I decided I'd chance them. The three guys in the bike section of the store told me that the boss wasn't there, the work schedule had been set and he wouldn't be back until eight thirty in the morning.

Even then there was no guarantee that it would get repaired first thing. I offered to give the mechanic a few quid bonus to come back and do it as he'd just walked out the door. The guys tried to raise him on the phone but failed.

I asked the guys if any of them could do the work, and when one of them nodded I offered him the same bribe to ignore the schedule and fix my bike as a matter of priority. The boys quickly divided the tasks for the rest of the day between each other and took my bike. I was delighted.

Getting the bike back an hour later brought my hopes of getting to London on time back on track. Rather than take the hour to drive back and restart the journey that evening, we decided to rest overnight and hit off before dawn so that I could roll past the accident site as dawn broke.

The plan was to reach Cambridge. It was a great plan. The only problem was my ankle. I'd obviously done it some form of damage in the fall yesterday, and it had swollen up. I did get a little kick out of one thing during the day: I passed through the tiny little village of New York, just sixteen kilometres outside the city of Boston in Lincolnshire.

I hadn't been allowed to cycle from New York to Boston earlier in the year in the US, but this unexpected turn of events gave me the chance to tick it off the bucket list, albeit not quite in the same form as I would have expected it starting out.

Late in the evening, as I approached Cambridge, Adam passed me with a toot of the horn. Then I heard a noise behind me and I spotted a rider approaching, absolutely flying by me in a high-end Pinarello that glistened with the same colours Bradley Wiggins had displayed in winning the Tour de France in 2012. The gap between us continued to grow, until I decided I wanted to catch him.

Despite the 170km already done that day, my ankle being twice the size it normally is, and not having my top gears, I didn't want to get beaten. I found the speedometer increasing slowly until I was settled around 35 KMph, then kept going as the gap began to shrink. The low-lying sun behind me was casting a lengthy shadow ahead of me, and when it began edging past him,

I saw him take a look over his shoulder.

His face gave his thoughts away completely. He was wondering how the guy he'd managed to fly by three kilometres ago managed to catch him. We fell in beside each other on the side road.

"How long is your ride?" he asked.

"Seventeen," I said, pausing while I added the distance done today to the amount I'd calculated this morning, "thousand, nine hundred and ninety four miles. So far."

His reaction again spoke volumes and as we reached the point we were going separate ways he stopped and fired off a load of questions about my ride. We chatted for a while, but I still had to get to Cambridge and daylight was becoming precious.

I stayed with Louise in Cambridge. We'd met in Fargo a month earlier and she invited me to stay for the night. The damage I'd done to my leg the previous day hadn't exactly helped matters on the bike today, and my ankle had blown up in a major way during the exertions of the day's ride. On the other hand, I'd managed to close the gap to a very manageable distance. I'd told people to expect me at lunch time in Greenwich in two days' time.

I was in a position to finish the next day, but I wanted to share the experience with my friends and family who'd gone to great lengths and expense to help me make it to the finish line. I planned on cycling to London this evening and make the short distance to Greenwich the following day as I'd promised people.

My second-last morning started with a radio interview with Morning Ireland on RTE about the feat already completed. All the while, my phone and social media accounts continued to blow up all day long as news outlets at home and abroad picked up on my pending achievement. Once the interview was done, Louise had prepared a breakfast, and I was ready to go.

I set my GPS for 'London, England' and the distance popped up as just over a hundred kilometres.

I was looking at my last real day on the bike. Tomorrow would be mostly ceremonial and for the benefit of my family and friends. The final day was pretty uneventful, Adam had been playing a blinder, and with his help I'd managed to close the gap to the finish line as I'd hoped.

I spent most of the day cycling along the canal bank, watching the city growing larger in my eye line, and before I knew it, I was dropping my bike to Adam's house in Shoreditch, giving me a scant eleven kilometre spin to Greenwich the following day. I left my bike at Adam's and set off across the city to visit my sister Ruth. I slept well and prepared for the emotion of the next day.

As I was picking up the bike the following morning, my family and a large number of friends were all in touch to confirm arrangements. I followed my original route across the capital as closely as possible. After cycling across Tower Bridge for the first time 490 days before, crossing it again after having cycled the entire way around the world brought on a burst of emotion from me. I'd said from the start that I knew it was possible for me to complete this challenge, but whether I'd truly believed it from the first day I'd considered it? I don't know.

Here I was, about to finish the World Cycle Race. I was the only person who started the event who would achieve that. Sixteen months earlier, with absolutely no competitive experience, I'd lined up at the start line of my first ever bicycle race and here I was, within a whisker of winning it.

Given the way the event had played out, there hadn't been a doubt that I would win the event for well over a year, but I was actually within touching distance of the finish line.

* * *

I arrived at the gates of Greenwich Park fifteen minutes before I'd expected to get there. I didn't want to arrive before the allotted hour, so I pulled up at a small mobile shop and ordered a drink. I spotted a friend, Brian Creegan, making his way towards the park, I called his name and he came over. He was worrying that he wouldn't make it to the observatory by the time I'd get there, so I promised I'd wait for him. Fifteen minutes later, I'd confirmed with my friend Damien that everyone I was expecting had arrived, so I set off up the short climb to the observatory which sits on the line which marks the start and end of time across the globe.

My family, friends and supporters dotted around the area in front of the observatory, and all I could focus on was the spontaneous cheering and applause as I rounded the final corner and made my way up to the finish line at the top of the straight.

I CROSSED THE FINISH LINE!

The previous five years flashed through my mind: the marathons, the dates, the gym sessions, the hours and hours in the saddle in preparation, the emails sent looking for support, and the faces of the people I'd met along the way. As I passed through the blue and white World Cycle Race signage I was elated. The next thing I knew, I fell into an embrace from my parents and my sister.

People milled around looking for photos and hugs. Damian, Brian, Sophie, Kevin & Marion, my cousin Collie are some of the faces I remember but I can't be sure who else was there. There were people who'd come on purpose and people who'd simply been in the park and had been pulled in by the noise and ceremony of the occasion.

The experience was now over, with a lifetime of memories that

I'd made over thirty thousand kilometres, twenty seven countries, forty four flat tyres, three robberies, three falls, and, most importantly, hundreds of thousands of people across the world having heard me talk about how "It's OK not to feel OK".

As the crowd drifted away, I looked around and I was back with just my family around me again. They started talking about plans for getting back to their hotel. I picked up the bike, swung my leg over the crossbar, and smiled.

"Enjoy your cab ride," I said. "I'll race you there!"

HOMECOMING

10th July - 11th July, 2015

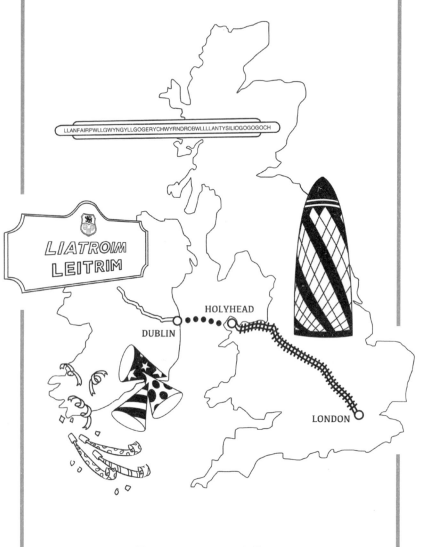

Distance: 166km

Elevation: 845 metres

58
EXHALE

The flashing lights of the police cars stopped traffic on both sides of the roundabout as we approached. A smile and a wave were forthcoming from the uniformed Garda as the train of cyclists behind me weaved around the traffic circle before picking up the road again on the other side. Less than two hours to go.

A week had passed since I'd crossed the finish line in Greenwich, and it had passed in a blur. The previous morning I'd left Dublin with some friends and supporters to make the final leg of the journey home to Leitrim.

My nephew Matthew was cycling beside me, almost a foot taller than when I'd started the cycle. In my absence, he'd developed from the boy who'd just about cycled to Longford with me sixteen months earlier.

With Matthew's youthful enthusiasm, he was itching to speed things up. He had struggled to complete the 40km distance the previous time on the road, but his return journey was spent trying to rein in his friends at the front of the peloton. Behind the boys, a collection of bodies merged into one large group as we passed through Newtownforbes, Rooskey and Dromod, eventually reaching Carrick on Shannon.

I was blown away by what awaited me at my final break at Trailblazers. There were people everywhere. Every time I turned around there was another congratulatory hug or hand shake. Some faces were very familiar; others I was seeing for the first time. It was above my wildest expectations.

I might have been back in Leitrim, but I wasn't home yet. I still had to negotiate the 6km that remained to complete my journey.

Fifteen minutes later, I stopped at the welcome signpost to Leitrim Village. The local photographer took a few pictures, and I took a few deep breaths before getting back in the saddle and allowing gravity to do its work one final time.

The entire cavalcade arrived at the local community centre to a phenomenal welcome. The car park was full of people of all ages. The entire village had come out to welcome me home. It was a reception normally reserved for a victorious football team.

The bunting, signs and music playing over the speakers created a party atmosphere. Teas, coffees, cakes, buns and biscuits were on tables around the room. I found myself shaking hands and sharing hugs with my neighbours and lifelong friends who appeared genuinely delighted to see me home safe and sound. I was posing for pictures with the children and signing autographs.

After the initial excitement of my arrival had worn off, I found myself standing quietly just inside the front door of the venue. The women of the community were serving hot drinks and buttered scones to the masses while the adults had found seats somewhere and were catching up with the rest of the local news.

Children played noisily around the room, trying to sneak as

many biscuits and cakes as possible while hiding how many they'd eaten from their parents.

From the small stage, the MC, Enda introduced me and while saying a few words I took the opportunity to thank everyone who had helped me in any way, shape or form.

I surveyed the room. An entire community were doing their little bit to acknowledge my achievement. They had not just played their part that day, but over my entire life.

"It takes a village to raise a child," says the old African proverb. That much was certainly true. Everyone in this village had helped to raise me.

My mind was drawn back to the afternoon, almost five years previous, when I'd lost sight of the support network I had all around me and almost made a decision that would have affected, in some way, every person in this room. Luckily, that was when I reached out and asked for help. When I did, the support of hundreds of people helped me to make the necessary positive changes to my life.

As the crowd started to thin out, our final thank you's and congratulations exchanged, I helped some of the kids collect the cups from around the room and made my own way outside to where I'd abandoned my bike.

It was four hundred metres, around the corner, to my parent's house. My bike wasn't going to cycle itself.

I strapped on my helmet and clipped my right foot into the pedal one last time and pushed off.

ACKNOWLEDGEMENTS

The limitations of space and my efforts to keep the story flowing mean that trying to fit the thousands of people who played a part in this cycle just isn't possible within the confines of these pages. That said, each and every person who played a part in this story, whether mentioned here or not, has a place in my heart forever.

I start with my parents; my mum has always been my biggest supporter. Without her, none of this would have been possible. My dad, in his own quiet way, was with me in spirit on the journey too. My sisters Kathy & Ruth are my best friends in the world and the next generation of Matthew and Charlie inspire me every day. Thank you all for just being yourselves.

In writing and compiling this book a number of people deserve a lot of credit. My editor Danny Gorny, illustrator Edel Feely, cover photographer Jesse Horrelbeke, typesetting and cover designer David Leeflang, and the numerous photographers who donated their images including Joseph Dixon, Lar Redmond, Paul O'Reilly, Kim Munday, Alan Mahon, Ryan Deveraux & Willie Donnellan. My many proof readers - I hope you enjoyed the sneak peek at the manuscript as much as I did sharing it with you.

A huge thank you to the partners and sponsors who played a vital role in helping me to prepare and maintain my body and my equipment during the cycle: Martin Kennedy, Cliodhna O'Connor, Daithi McCabe, Conor Clifford, Kevin Croke, Colin Griffin, Daniel Davey, and Sean Kinane.

Mike Hall, Simon Hutchinson, Juliana Burhing, Vin Cox, Gerry Duffy, Niall Breslin, Colm (Hayes) Caffrey, Rob Carley & Maghnus Collins each in their own way inspired me to pursue my dreams and cycle around the planet.

Vicki Notaro & Yvonne Hogan in FIT Magazine, Orlagh Marnane, Mark Burke and Karen Howley in AerTV, Rob Harnett in Sport For Business, Maria Connaughton in Spin11, the entire team in Cycleways and James Keating of LandsLeaving Media.

My support team included Sara Rothwell and Louise Loughlin, my sister Ruth who picked up the baton in Munich, and Adam Browne who joined me for the final days to the finish line.

A huge thank you to all the journalists around the planet who covered the story of my cycle and allowed me the platform to spread the suicide prevention message that I carried with me.

To the fantastic people who invited me to speak about my journey in their schools, community groups, churches, universities, work places and sports stadiums.

The people who showed faith in me and my message along the way. Everyone who supported the crowdfunding campaign, cycled a bit of the way, offered a bed, meal or even just conversation I can never fully repay each of you for your goodness and generosity. In that respect I especially want to thank my parents Joe & Beth Earley, my grandmother Veronica McCarthy RIP, John Mullen, Version 1, Terry North, Margaret Cox, Eamon Harbison, Dermod McCarthy, Padraic Carney, Alan Taylor, Seamus Butler, David Malone, Jimmy & Lily Roche, Jeannette Gibbs, Moyna Trodden, Pauline O'Shaughnessy, Jason Tompkins, Dr. Kathy Gray, Alma Mackin, Kevin Boland, Niamh Ward, Edel Harbison, Paul McGovern, Joe & Eilish Beirne, Alex Dizon, Brian & Barbara Healy, Maire & the late Paddy O'Carroll RIP, Ann O'Connell, Alan McCarthy, Michelle Serpa, Chiara Francesco, Cian Farrell,

Colin Simpson, Damien McLoughlin, Derek Scanlon, Gerry Duffy, Padraic Hallinan, James Whitney, Karl Griffin, Mark Rohan, Michael Taheny, Noel Boyle, Noel Hayes, Paul Farrell, Brid McEvoy, Christina Lacey, Damian Riordan, Mike McCarthy, Noel Farrell, Patrick Kennedy, Carolyn & Charles Hansen, Paul McCann, Sarah Barrett, Trevor Graham, Donal Kennedy, Liam Harbison, Enda McDonagh, Darren Conway, Ciaran Tansey, Verona Riots, Paddy McKenna, Mulligan's of Sandymount, Neil O'Donnell, Noel Hickey, Hugh Gibbons, Conal & Stephanie Gibbons, Gerard & Damian Lynch in Trailblazers, Fiachra O'Mathuna, Seamus Gibbons & Leonard Costello, Martin Cook and everyone else who supported me. Unfortunately I don't have enough space here to list all 800+ supporters of the campaign.

The people who offered beds, food or entertainment along the way were Tommy Moran, The Crown Hotel London, Franziska Kuhne, Prasad Erande, Mark Chowter, Spiceroads, Grainne & Richard Styles, Alan Taylor, Chantelle Mader, David of Prideau's of Margaret River, Cathie Denehy, Pauline Robinson, Leon & Maureen Clarke, Ronald & Belinda Freund, Rick & Amanda Kehoe, Sile Murray & Michael Bungate, Stan, Karen, Ellen & Mia Soroka, Deirdre Hopkins, Base Backpackers, Miriam Bielski, Fergal & Sarah, Greg and Suzi Bell, Lisa Csima, Darren & Eri Carney, Sinead McKenna, Sean McKenna, Sarah Farrell & Phil Pepper, Sandra & John-Darragh, Nollaig & Josh Trevarthen, Andy Hunt, Natural High, Nick Tracey, Hugh Gibbons, Jillian Boland, The Boland family, Jono Crute, Daniel Patman, Bryan & Berry Staub, Jim Moran, Danielle Austin, Fergus Whitney, Martin Silke, Brandy Montez, Tom, Kim-Lilly & Hannah Hansen, Rory O'Driscoll, Aisling Toolan, Stephanie Roche & Dean Zambra, Gordon Hanlon & Kathy Grafflin Cholette, Charles & Carolyn Hansen, Lynn Bradley, Lillie & Jimmy Roche, Gerry and Rosemarie Flood & family, Padraic & Alison Carney, Michelle &

Mark Serpa, Alix Mac, Paul McGovern, Cycle Against Suicide, Lisa Petrie, Noble Argue, Lou Shackleton & Paul Simpson, Adam & Sinead Browne.

The cyclists I picked up along the way included Franziska Kuhne, Richard Styles, Will van Rompaey, Maria & Zigor, Stephen Grey & Kane Stevenson, Bryan Staub, Martin Valldeby, Kevin Cunniffe and the send-off and homecoming peletons that joined me to finish and end the journey.

To the entire community of Leitrim Village and the surrounding area: coming home to such a phenomenal welcome made me really appreciate home and the people who make it such a special place. I'm so proud to call this beautiful part of the world my home.

To my friends in Cycle Against Suicide & Pieta House, thank you for the support and the chats at all hours of the day and night. Your messages and thoughts of support carried me across the deserts, plains and mountains along the way.

Once again, thank you to each and every person who played a part in the entire story over the last six years. I love you all. I hope you enjoyed reading this account of those years as much as I have living them.